W9-BJC-742

MIRACLES
IN THE
MIDDLE

MIRACLES IN THE MIDDLE

Men Who Live the Promise in Midlife

RICH BIMLER

TED SCHROEDER

CPH.
SAINT LOUIS

Scripture quotations marked NRSV are from the New Revised Standard Version of the Bible, copyright © 1989. Used by permission.

All Scripture quotations, unless otherwise indicated, are taken from the HOLY BIBLE, NEW INTERNATIONAL VERSION®. NIV®. Copyright © 1973, 1978, 1984 by International Bible Society. Used by permission of Zondervan Publishing House. All rights reserved.

Copyright © 1997 Concordia Publishing House
3558 S. Jefferson Avenue, St. Louis, MO 63118-3968
Manufactured in the United States of America

All rights reserved. No part of this publication may be reproduced, stored in a retrieval system, or transmitted, in any form or by any means, electronic, mechanical, photocopying, recording, or otherwise, without the prior written permission of Concordia Publishing House.

Library of Congress Cataloging-in-Publication Data

Schroeder, Theodore W., 1939–
    Miracles in the middle : men who live the promise in midlife / Theodore W. Schroeder, Richard W. Bimler
        p.   cm.
    ISBN 0-570-04890-7
    1. Middle aged men—Religious life. 2. Christian life—Lutheran authors.
I. Bimler, Richard. II. Title.
    BV4528.2.S37   1997
    248.8'42—dc21   96-44487
                                                           CIP

2   3   4   5   6   7   8   9   10   06 05 04 03 02 01 00 99

For Ellen Schroeder and Hazel Bimler—
wives extraordinaire!
Thanks for the memories—
before, during, and even after
our midlife years together.

Contents

Introduction

My midlife adventure starts with a story:

Have you had your midlife crisis yet?" came the question from the earnest young man sitting across from me at lunch. I'd taken him to lunch to get acquainted with him. He was, it seemed, going to be my assistant for the next year.

"What did you say?" I responded. At 50, my hearing sometimes plays tricks on me.

He plunged ahead. "I mean, everyone has one. We studied that in adult development class. About your age (this phrase he said with a particular emphasis on the word *your*) people go through an identity crisis not unlike that of the adolescent years. Emotional turmoil, behavioral aberrations—you know. All of that stuff."

I began to feel like a laboratory animal being readied for dissection. "No. I don't think so," I said. "Things seem to be about the same as before."

"Really? No desires to run off with a younger woman? No crisis of confidence? No thought about escaping to a desert island?"

"Not really. I do occasionally think about a fishing trip to a lake in Minnesota, and once in a while I take my daughter out to lunch. But no South Sea island seems to come to mind."

He was clearly crestfallen. "Well, never mind," he said rather bruskly. "Maybe yours is just delayed. But believe me, it's coming." On the last phrase his face shone with a kind of prophetic light.

I thought that perhaps I was supposed to apologize for my lack of a crisis, but the fact that I did not fit his expectation made me feel so good, I almost forgot about the midlife whatever I was dealing with.

I had told him that I was not having a midlife crisis. Certainly, that was true. I had dealt with many crises in my life—some of them life-threatening. I had worked through my own battle with cancer and sat at the bedside of my wife as she struggled to survive a ruptured appendix. I had run to be with a young wife who had just lost her only child in an accident and held many a hand of a person on the way to a dangerous operation. I knew what crises were like. Crises were always sudden and encompassing, demanding instant action. They were almost always matters of life and death. They always mustered dramatic emotions—adrenaline surges sparked by fear. If crises were persons, they would be looming assassins, setting upon us with fierce immediacy.

I didn't tell my inquisitive young friend, but I was dealing with something having to do with the middle of my life. The word crisis, however, would not describe it.

I can still remember my first real date when I was 16. Now *there* was a crisis. I stood in front of her door, polished and perfumed, convinced that I was about to enter a five-hour trial of tongue-tied silence that would inevitably doom me to social rejection and scorn for the rest of my life. The memory brings beads of perspiration to my forehead. This midlife thing is nothing like that. It isn't sharp and angular and sudden, like real crises are. It has nothing to do with life and death, produces no surge of adrenaline, seems to ask no immediate response. It feels, I don't know, sort of seductively uncomfortable. If a crisis is like a looming assassin, this is more like a lingering houseguest.

This thing, this whatever-it-is, is certainly real. I can easily identify its characteristics. It has something to do with sitting, staring at the television, and not knowing what to do to overcome the sense of emptiness that envelopes me. It has to do with the back-of-the-mind awareness that there are no other sounds in the house in the evening. It is something like the realization that Monday morning is always "another" Monday morning, stacked neatly upon all the rest. If adolescence had to do with great peaks and valleys of emotion, this is more a kind of perpetual plateau—a flatness to the passing of the days.

Midlife crisis this is not. This is more like a muddle.

When I was eight, my brothers and I had a thing for

mud. We found mud, made mud with the hose in the backyard, built forts with mud, and generally drove my mother to distraction as she tried to keep us, our clothes, and the house clean. We had one favorite mud place, a kind of a huge puddle that never seemed to dry up, even in the hottest of summers. Like a siren the puddle called us. We took off our shoes and waded into the tepid water, savoring the soft, cool mud between our toes. And we dared one another to stand still—just to feel ourselves sinking deeper and deeper into the mud, knowing that at some point the hold of the dark goo under the surface of the water would hold us fast and we'd not be able to get out again.

My mother called to us futilely as we left the house on Saturday. "Don't you kids go near that mud puddle."

In time, mud puddle became muddle.

"Should we go to the muddle?" my brother asked.

"We're not supposed to," I replied.

"Come on! I dare you!"

And of course we stood in our muddle, placing our bare feet into the clutches of the demons of the mud that might not let us go.

This midlife thing was a little like that—like a seductive mud puddle. Kind of warm and comfortable, tempting us always to sit still, to vegetate on the couch in front of a football game, wondering if we'd ever be able to move again. The muddle tempts us to give in to the demons of ooze in the middle of life that would take us into old age before we even have a chance to protest.

My young friend could never understand it, but this something is all soft and mushy, all shapeless and dingy.

Galloping regrets trouble our sleep. Long-forgotten fears and frustrations pull at the edges of our awareness. Broken dreams clutter the landscape and much of what we tried to build has turned into rubble. We face a bleak future and try to avoid gazing into an if-only past.

Maybe if this thing were a crisis we could do something about it. But this muddle doesn't seem to have a way out. We don't know how we got into this mess or how we should get out. Standing still only gets us in deeper.

What do we do now?

Ted

The time in one's life affectionately titled "Midlife Crisis" can be something like adolescence. It can arouse many negative thoughts, feelings, and perceptions. These stages in our lives are often labeled "problem times" and people deal with us as though we have contracted a horrible disease.

But whether we are in the age range for a "midlife crisis attack" or we are teenagers dealing with struggles and challenges of life, the *given* for each of us is that we continue to be loved and forgiven in Christ Jesus!

It is God's presence in our lives that is the constant rather than problems, pains, and frustrations. And it is because the Lord is a daily part of our lives that we can deal positively with being "over the hill," or at least nearing the top of that hill.

Midlife. Does that mean our life is half over or we still

have half of an exciting life to live? It reminds me of the comedian and the half glass of water: "Is it half full or half empty?" he asks. The response: "That's not the point at all. The point is that it's too big a glass!"

The Lord has given us a full life to live whether that life is 50, 80, or 120 years. (I often wonder how Methuselah dealt with his midlife crises at such an old age.)

We have a tendency to focus too much on our age and the changes taking place, and not enough on the presence of the Lord and His daily renewing of us through Word and Sacrament. "This is the day the LORD has made," says the psalmist (Psalm 118:24). And He's been doing a pretty good job of it each day of our lives.

Both Ted and I lost our fathers when they were in their 50s. We missed many years with them. They didn't even have the chance of experiencing some of the midlife crises that their sons are now going through. Perhaps we could have learned more from them than we did. We both have a strong sense of longing, wishing these important men were still with us and that we could learn more from them. But we did not share those years with them. And rather than bemoaning the fact that they are not here, we can thank the Lord that other men around us have been able to share their lives and experiences with us. And we can also thank the Lord for our dads' lives and the effects they had on various people.

Rich

In this book, we intend to do nothing other than answer "What do we do now?" But we are not experts offering a surefire "do it yourself" strategy guaranteed to instantly turn midlife into a positive experience. Instead, we offer the insights of two who are coming through the crisis, trying to see it from a spiritual point of view as an opportunity for new life instead of a call to self-defeating busy-ness.

These pages reveal stories, perceptions, anecdotes, and feelings about our life in the Lord, focusing on some of the struggles, challenges, and joys in the lives of men aged 40 to 60. This book will not tell you what to do, how to solve your problems, how to make sure you are a better husband, father, or grandfather, but we hope it will bring a strong Gospel word of hope, promise, and encouragement to each reader.

We invite you to look with us at some of the sticking places that we all encounter as we muddle through the middle of our lives. Some are humorous, some deadly serious. But we are convinced that when we cling to the gift of victory in Jesus Christ, when we stare our fears and frustrations in the face, when we move forward with our lives, acting positively in hope, we can move out of the muddle and into life that opens us, challenges us, and invites us into the light of God's grace.

So this is a book of hope—mutual hope—hope that we share. It is a book of resurrection because we believe that in every tomb of fear or doubt, in every ending, in every sticking place, God creates new life. It is a book of celebration because we are new each day.

We don't have all the answers. We have not completely overcome our own muddles. We don't offer a quick fix but we invite you on a tour with us. Walk with us through this muddle. See it for what it is, and join us as we turn to God's promises for the spiritual power that can turn even the muddle in the middle into an opportunity for abundant living.

Today, Lord, we thank You for life itself. We thank You for the opportunities to be living long enough to experience some midlife crises. And we thank You for Your Spirit who continues to be present as we work at joining the "over the hill" club.

ONE

Who Are These Men Who Live the Promise in Midlife?

To get a better view of who we midlife men are, let's look at some recent statistics. A study commissioned by *Modern Maturity* recently subdivided Americans into seven life-stage segments. The younger segments include:

1. "Nervous Novices," median age 30, who are united by the relative lack of life experiences.

2. "Clock Watchers," median age 32, who are trying to get ahead while coping with young-adult transitions such as job changes and divorces.

3. "First Families," median age 37, who are dual-income, full-nest, married-couple households.

4. "Second Chancers," median age 45, who have begun a second life after a major transition caused by external events. Most of these people have divorced and remarried, while 37 percent have made a major career change and 31 percent have lost a job. The values of this group are refocused on family life.

5. "Continuing Caregivers," median age 55, who still have dependents. Seventy-two percent had an adult child move back home, 66 percent provide day care to a grandchild, and 46 percent care for a parent. Their lifestyle is one of extreme busy-ness and they are willing to spend more for quality and convenience.

6. "New Me," median age 55, who have experienced an internal change such as midlife crisis, major career change, major change in diet, or major illness. They have the optimism of survivors, but are made cautious by their past. Incidentally, they also tend to be the most health-conscious of all the groups and most likely to be offended by negative stereotypes of older people.

7. "Free Birds," median age 69, who are likely to be retired and free of family obligations. They can concentrate on their own wants and needs, and many no doubt play the role of "snow birds" in southern climates during the winter months.

What does all this mean for us midlife folks? First, it shows that our society has conveniently created a niche for each of us. The danger here is the assumption that just because I am a certain age, I automatically have all the characteristics of everyone else that age. Part of our struggle in living out God's promise for us is not to succumb to a society that brands us and locks us into negative attitudes and lifestyles.

Men who live the promise of God in midlife are those who can observe and learn from others, look at current statistics and trends with objective eyes, and still keep focused on the spiritual values and truths that God continues to set before us. Whether you fit into the "New Me" segment or the "Second Chancers" is beside the point. The point is that the Lord provides gifts, blessings, and opportunities in our lives for us to live and share the promise of health and hope with others.

We can rejoice in the changes that are taking place in our daily lives. Rather than view these changes as problems or crises, we can help each other accept and deal with them forthrightly and with hope-filled eyes. I'm reminded of a 45-year-old father who said, "I know my kids are growing up because they have stopped asking me where they came from and now refuse to tell me where they are going!"

It is this kind of attitude, this kind of life value that does not try to erase the struggles and concerns we have in our lives, but deals with these challenges in a light-hearted and hope-filled manner. My guess is that this father, struggling to communicate with his kids, is also communicating love, hope, and forgiveness as he deals with specific concerns. He is living out God's promise to him during his midlife years.

DOWN WITH GROAN-UPS!

Remember the days when you couldn't wait to "grow up," to be older, just like your big brother?

Now that I've hit the coveted "over 50" group, I sometimes reflect on how fun my childhood was. But I'm glad I am the age that I am. I would not wish to be a teenager in today's world. And I'm not that enthralled with reliving the "good old days." I'm not sure how good they really were.

There is no such thing as a "grown up." We continue to grow in the Lord and in our relationships with others daily. Perhaps part of the midlife crisis syndrome is our assumption that we have finished growing and there is nothing more to do than get old and fade away.

I'll say it again: I like the age I am right now. And I will like the age I am 10 years from now, 15 years from now, and even 25 years from now. As I continue to struggle with the regrets I have because of what I did or didn't do years ago, I can also rejoice that the Lord is still in control of my life. He will provide opportunities for me to grow spiritually, physically, mentally, and emotionally. As the bumper sticker says, "God's not done with me—yet!" And I'm not done with Him either!

Perhaps we need a bumper sticker that says, "Down with groan-ups!" If growing older means more groaning and moaning, leave me out. But if "growing up" really means continuing to grow in excitement, knowledge, and experiences, count me in.

I recently read that as we grow older, our "real" behaviors and values become more obvious. Perhaps we need to review daily our attitudes and behaviors. Am I getting grouchier, less communicative, more impatient, less understanding? Or, am I able to take myself more lightly, enjoy the little things in life, and keep my problems and pains in perspective? I suggest we each reflect on our behavior to see if it is a reflection of who we really are.

Down with groan-ups! Up with life! Let's continue "growing-up" together.

FOR REFLECTION OR DISCUSSION

1. What does it mean to you to be called a "midlifer"? What does that stage in your life mean to you now? What are you looking forward to?

2. How do you understand the phrase "God is not done with me"? What purpose do you see God setting out for you? How will you respond?

3. What struggles remain for you? Share some of them with other midlifers. What encouragement can you give to one another? What help can you find in your relationship with God in Jesus Christ?

TWO

Matters of Death and Life

The Cave

Growing boys create a world of wonders on which to hang their imaginations. Our neighborhood was no different. We boasted the standard attractions. We had our "haunted house" (an abandoned farm house, as I recall); we had our balding, lemon-faced "grouch" (who may have had reason to be grouchy, given the tribe of eight- to 10-year-old marauders in the area); we had our "fort" (a muddy hole in the ground) and our "tree house"—and many other attractions. One of our favorites was *the cave*.

In retrospect, I don't think it was much of a cave. It was probably more of a denlike indentation in a nearby limestone bluff. But the bearless lair (though the largest wildlife in the area was a muskrat, we were sure a bear

23

had been there) was a great place to make-believe. In our wonderful cave, we were Indians resting from the hunt, or we were the Jesse James gang fooling the posse, or explorers searching for buried treasure. Happy memories all. But the cave was different from many of the other neighborhood attractions. For an imaginative lad, entering the cave alone (even on a dare) could bring on real neck-crawling terror. To this day, the thought of moving through that dark opening into the black expanse beyond brings an adrenaline rush that makes my heart race. And whenever a sudden damp smell reaches my nose, I am transported into my eight-year-old body, crouching at the entrance to the cave. I feel the looming darkness. I hear the deafening silence.

I fell into that cave again the other evening. It just happened. I was at home, doing my usual thing. I had mailed another check to one of the kids at college, listened to my mother complain on the phone that I had not called recently, sat through a couple of painfully unfunny programs on TV, and given my wife a good-night peck as she headed upstairs.

The television nagged me, so I silenced it. The lamp light pressed on my eyes, so I turned it off. Suddenly, before I realized it, I was a child in that cave again, and I was afraid.

The silence hurt my ears. I strained to hear the sound of children moving in their bedrooms, but the rooms were empty. I longed to hear someone call to me a reminder about the car keys or the next day's lunches. But I heard no sound that said I was needed. Not a murmur pulled me into the life of those who loved me. There in my cave, I could not even break the silence with the sound of my own voice.

The darkness paralyzed me. I huddled in a blackness that blanketed my thoughts, my dreams, my future. And then from somewhere in my memory the cold, damp smell of the cave filled my nose. Or was it the smell of the cave? Was it really a creation of my memory? Was it the smell of my childhood? Or was it the smell of the future? The smell of the dark days ahead? The smell of my own tomb?

For a long time, I could not move. I could hardly breathe. I felt the hard beating of my heart and realized that it could not beat forever. Like a lost child, I wept for someone to come into the cave and bring a lamp and sit with me and hold me and tell me that it would be all right.

But will it be? Will the silence continue to envelope me? Will the darkness cover me? Will the smell of my passing years be the terrible, damp, lonely smell of my own tomb?

"IN THE MIDST OF LIFE, WE ARE IN DEATH ... "

That troubling phrase is often read at graveside committal services. When we are young, the thought is easy to ignore. As we grow older, the words become more pressing. Death inexorably draws nearer. It lurks in the sharp pain in our chest and hides just under that sudden dizzy spell. And its nearness brings no comfort. Death is the thief, the destroyer, the raider who threatens to seize all we hold dear. Death is the cave of darkness that we enter alone—and there is no outlet.

"He was only 40 and the heart attack took him."

"Right in her prime—cancer again."

"No one expected it. Some kind of infection. He didn't have a chance."

"A person like that, so energetic and full of life. How could that happen?"

With morbid curiosity we read the death notices in the paper. How young was he? What finally got him? What are my chances?

As the years pass, death is no longer a distant specter but a gloomy pall. Uninvited, death invades our very life and lurks just beyond our awareness.

We see loved ones die. We may have lived our first 30 or 40 years without experiencing the death of someone close to us, but in our mid years and later, death snatches those we hold dear.

Death signs our body. We feel the pains of age, see age spots, watch our hair fall out, watch wrinkles form. In a real way, we put on the face and figure of death long before we actually stop breathing. And the mirror will not let us forget.

Death shadows our future. Broken dreams litter the landscape we have set out for ourselves and each day threatens to become the end bracket of life.

"I don't know what's the matter with me," my friend said. "I have everything anyone would want. I own my own business. It is a remarkable success. I have a wife and grown children—all well and doing fine. I'm respected in the community. I can afford to buy whatever I want. And still I'm so unhappy. I wake every morning and it is all I can do just to get out of bed. Life seems so empty, so meaningless, so … dead."

All of us who are coming through the middle of life know what my friend is talking about. Doctors describe that feeling with words such as "depression." Social scientists blame the emptiness on the transitions of midlife, the readjusting of our dreams, the changes in our bodies, the slowing of our mental and physical processes, and more.

But for those of us who are in it, who are living through midlife—who find ourselves in the muddle in the middle of life—death has become our companion and has made itself at home in our vision, our hopes, our dreams, our view of ourselves, our relationships, our future, our very life. And sometimes we can hardly get out of bed in the morning.

WHAT WON'T WORK

Death has staying power. A number of the courses of action prescribed to get death out of our life will not work:

1. Self-resurrection will not work. The old German fable about Baron Munchausen tells how the Baron saved himself and his horse from drowning by putting a strap under the horse and, while sitting on the horse's back, lifting them both out of the water. Attempts to resurrect ourselves will probably work about as well. Though it is certainly true that simply sitting in a pool of our own self-pity or cowering in the face of our own impending death will do nothing but narrow life and push us farther into depression, it is also true that "making up our

mind" to be more alive will not suddenly open our lives to rebirth, free from the specter of death. We cannot climb out of the cave by ourselves.

2. Pretending will not work. Some people solve problems using the "let's not look at it and maybe it will go away" approach. Others use the "if I get high enough or busy enough I won't have to think about it" tactic. Neither will work. Ignoring, in fact, only makes meeting death more difficult when it happens.

3. Positive thinking will not chase death away. Thinking positively about ourselves, our lives, and our future certainly will help—especially if we are caught in fits of gloom. But positive thinking that does not reach to our inner selves is only wishful thinking.

LIVING INTO THE RESURRECTION

All good intentions, dreams, plans, actions, activities aside, we are in the midst of life and in the midst of death at the same time. That is who we are. There is nothing that we can do to change the reality of our human condition. Thinking right thoughts won't do it. Working to create a new body won't do it. Pretending we are young won't do it. We live on the edge of death and as we grow older, that edge grows ever nearer. We have no control over the margin of life.

But we do have control over what we do about the encroaching robber. Surely we can sit and feel sorry for ourselves, or try to pretend it away, or get so busy we don't have time to think about it. We can deny it (never say the word). Or, we can attempt to make light of it: "I've called in sick too often. Today, I'm calling in dead." But none of those changes the reality that death increasingly has hold of us.

The "help" for our dying is outside ourselves.

St. Paul, moving toward the end of his own life, was able to cry: " 'Where, O death, is your victory? Where, O death, is your sting?' The sting of death is sin, and the power of sin is the law. But thanks be to God! He gives us the victory through our Lord Jesus Christ" (1 Corinthians 15:55–57).

When we are young, our faith relationship with God may be a fallback resource we save for times of trouble. It may be something we take for granted, or reflect on only occasionally. But as we grow older, we realize how temporary all the things that filled our younger eyes were and how important eternal things have become.

The old man sat bent over the table in his crumbling farm house. He spoke in a near whisper. "This old house is falling down," he said. "The roof leaks and the foundation is crumbling. And my body is going with it. I can barely walk anymore. The steps are too high for me. But if it crumbles to dust, if this old house and this old body go back to the earth they came from—what we built together, my Ellie and me, will not die. What we made together by the grace of God will last forever."

Forever. What do we have that has forever in it?

Certainly nothing we create for ourselves. Nothing we can dream or do or make or imagine has forever in it. Forever belongs to God and in Christ, forever is His gift to us.

We stand in terror of our own death. The cave waits for us. We cannot change it or undo it or disarm it or destroy it. We cannot overcome it or make it go away. "But thanks be to God! He gives us the victory through our Lord Jesus Christ" (1 Corinthians 15:57).

And because He has given the victory, we can live the resurrected life right now.

LIVING OUTSIDE THE CAVE

Life goes on. Time marks us. Death creeps in. But we who are given the victory are also given the challenge to live it. Without creating a Pollyanna world of make-believe, without playing psychological games with ourselves, without creating false hopes out of wishful thinking, we can live the resurrected life now.

Paul tells us that we know we were baptized into Jesus' death so that we might be a part of His resurrection now and "walk in newness of life" (Romans 6:4 NRSV). Walking in that newness means living in the confidence (sometimes shaken by doubt, and certainly not dependent on our strength) that nothing "in all creation [not even death], will be able to separate us from the love of God that is in Christ Jesus our Lord" (Romans 8:39).

In Christ, we can offer each other encouragement to live outside the cave, to be aware that in the middle of a muddle in the middle of our lives there is still hope and peace and joy. Even as we write, we occasionally find ourselves in our own caves of doubt and fear. We cannot claim to offer all the ways to joyful living. We still slosh around in our own muddles all too often. But we know that there is a way through the muddle. There is not an eternal seal on the cave door. The Spirit brings help for those times of doubt and despair. We know that all things are subject to the victory won for us in Jesus Christ.

And so we celebrate. We look at each day as a gift, each morning as renewal, each new year as an opportunity to be faced with hope. And with that hope we can encourage one another.

FOR REFLECTION OR DISCUSSION

1. Think of one time when death seemed very real. Tell about it. What did it feel like? What emotions were you aware of? Where did new life and hope come from?

2. Read 1 Corinthians 1–5. Reflect on or share what the message of the chapters means to you.

3. We are called "Easter People." What does that title mean to you? How would others see that title on your life?

4. Read Romans 8:28–29. What does that assurance mean to you as you think about your future? What gift do you see in the promise? How does the promise offer freedom?

A RESURRECTION ACTION

Surprise yourself (and others who watch you): Do at least one thing every day this week that no one would expect you to do—something celebratory, healing, helpful. Make it an adventure. Try something outrageous. Laugh. Then share your actions and reactions with someone else.

THREE

A
Matter
of Attitude

Where Are You Going?

Grandson Matthew was having a great time running up and down the halls of our new home. Without much furniture in it, he was able to run and jump and zip up and down the stairs of our new two-story. As I observed his coming and going, I tried to slow him down. When I finally was able to grab him, I looked at him as he panted and smiled and asked, "Where are you going?"

Matthew caught his breath, looked at me and said, "I don't know!"

There, in that fleeting moment, three-year-old Matthew had captured the question his grandpa has been struggling with for a number of years: "Where am I going?" And now, in the simple words of a child, this

question came back to haunt me. What was I doing with
my life? With the years that I have left, what difference
can I make? What are my priorities, really? And to most
of these questions I must confess I need to respond, "I
don't know!"

One thing I was sure of: I was committed to spending as much time as possible with Matthew and any other
grandchildren to come. I wanted to do for them some of
the things I did not do for my own three kids. I wanted
to ease the regret in my life for not spending as much
time as I thought I should have with Diane, Bob, and
Mike as they were growing and running and developing
as adolescents. (I don't always have an answer to "Where
am I going?" but I know that I want my grandchildren
around me as I go.)

HISTORY REVISITED

Many of us are perhaps trying to find out where we
are going by revisiting some of our mistakes and hopes
of the past. This is not all bad, as we strive to reach our
goals and enjoy the life the Lord has given to us. It can
become a problem, however, if we see that our main
purpose in life is to relive our mistakes. Our earlier days
are history. Our goofs and messes are things of the past.
The Lord brings health and healing to us each day with
His marvelous love and forgiveness in His proclamation,
"They are new every morning; great is Your faithful-
ness" (Lamentations 3:23).

It is really refreshing to know that we live on "this
side" of the resurrection, that all of our Good Fridays in
life have been met with Christ's Easter. So in some ways,

it's okay to answer the question "Where am I going?" with "I don't know." We certainly do not know the future, but one thing is sure: The Lord is already there, making way for us to celebrate our life in Him every day, starting with today.

Have you ever made a list of things you wish you had done in your past? Here are a few of mine:

1. I wish I would have known my dad much better before he died at age 50.

2. I wish I would have spent much more time with my three kids as they were growing up.

3. I wish I could have had more quality time with my wife during the early years of our marriage.

4. I wish my mother could have spent more time with my kids while they were growing up.

5. I wish I would have "thought out loud" more with my kids and others.

I wish, I wish, I wish. And the list goes on. It is interesting to note that all of the above wishes deal with relationships. Note too that none of these wishes can come true anymore. So why the list? To learn from the past and move on to today and tomorrow.

Where are you going? Are you attempting to relive your wishes, even though most of them can never be fulfilled? Instead, watch the Lord at work in you, allowing new relationships to develop and old relationships to be strengthened. I can't spend more time with my dad, but I can see the Lord moving me into some neat relationships with my grandkids, wife, and others around me. I can't relive the past, but I can learn from it and see that the Lord can make me new again.

God, in Christ Jesus, makes "Where am I going?" make sense. And even on days when I answer "I don't know," He continues to provide hope, forgiveness, and a sense of purpose in my life because of what He has already done for me.

Perhaps my role today is to be the best 54-year-old I can be. The past cannot be undone, but the future is wide open and is a gift from the Lord. I'm reminded of a coffee mug that says, "Life is hard—then you die." True, that's one way to go through life, sipping on your coffee and waiting for bad things to happen until death takes you. Maybe we need a new coffee mug: "Life is hard—but Easter has already happened!"

So where is your life taking you? What things in your past are you trying to undo or redo? Now is the time to see that the Lord has already allowed you to come to grips with these struggles. We don't have all the answers yet, but Christ has put us on the right track to renew and relive a life of joy, peace, and forgiveness in the days ahead.

SENDING "REGRETS"

Many of us continue to deal with regrets and unfulfilled dreams in our lives. To which of these can you relate?

I regret that

- I accepted that new position (or did not accept it).

- I didn't finish my schooling.
- We moved away from our family.
- I didn't listen more to my own kids.
- I didn't save more money for later years.
- I didn't become more active in my congregation and community.

RSVP

How do you respond to these and other regrets?

I find it helpful to remind myself that I cannot undo my past decisions and that I must deal with them. I also remind myself that our Lord has forgiven me for all the messes I have made in my life. Forgiveness is what keeps us going. I've always had trouble with the adage "forgive and forget." I still have trouble forgetting some of my blunders. I like the banner that says, "Forgiving is remembering, and then moving on!" To know a Lord who forgives and moves us along is the key to dealing with our regrets.

We will never be able to go back and make a new beginning, but we can start today and make a new ending.

ON THE SHORES WITH THE WAVES

I am writing these pages on the shores of Camp Arcadia on the east coast of Lake Michigan. The gentle waves lapping the sandy beach flow endlessly from their unknown sources. Where are they going? Do they know? I sometimes feel like a wave, flowing continually to the shore, making a little noise, and then disappearing onto the beach. What difference does one more wave make? Who really cares?

But there is a calm about the seashore. Every wave does its best to make at least a little noise, a little dent in the soft sand. And each wave, I suspect, carries with it a little bit of history—sand immersed in the wave itself, quietly molding smooth rocks beneath it.

Where am I going?

I too am lapping up life, loving the journey, celebrating with the wind how high I can splash, and bringing my own stories to the shores for anyone wanting to see and listen to them.

Waves seem to be part of a forgiving community. They need each other. They touch and play, and go their way. With the sun's light they sparkle—lights on the water providing a great view of God's creation. I suspect some waves don't sparkle, just like me when I am burned out, wishing I were going in a different direction from all the rest.

Where are we going? We are flowing into tomorrow, and into the next day, with some directions set and others just beginning.

FOR REFLECTION OR DISCUSSION

1. Think of some regrets that you can revisit. How can you save for the future, begin a new relationship with your son or friend, move to another city, continue your schooling, or change jobs? Are any of these things possible, or are they things to chalk up as history?

2. Write a letter of encouragement to a friend who needs affirmation. Write a letter to yourself—what do you need to hear from others?

3. Call a friend on the phone, just to visit. Listen to each other. Share regrets, joys, and frustrations and offer to call again soon.

4. Keep looking for stories and cartoons and newspapers and publications with which you can identify. Save them. Post them. Share them. Enjoy them.

What We Can Learn from Dogs, Cats, and Grandchildren

Some midlifer once quipped that life really begins when all the children move out and the dog dies. That might be a simplistic view of things, but there are those who feel that once children, pets, and other "annoying" phases of our life disappear, real living can begin.

What a sad view of life. During our midyears, we may need alone time to enjoy ourselves, others, and the gifts of creation, but we also need to stay tuned in to what children, grandchildren, and even pets can share with us.

Case in point: The phone just rang as I'm frantically

working on this manuscript. It's my seven-year-old grandson, Matthew, who wants me to come over right now to give him my opinion "on a couple of things." Even though I am trying to get this writing assignment finished, I had no trouble saying, "Sure, I'll be over in a little while!"

To be truthful, when this happened 20 years ago, when Matthew's mom called my office to ask if I could come home early to do something with her, I said, "Diane, I'd like to, but I've just got too much to do. Maybe we can do it some other time."

I am a slow learner, but one of the many things my grandchildren have taught me is the importance of responding to their needs and showing them that they are a priority in my life. My grandkids have taught me so many things: not to take life so seriously, how to forgive, to speak more honestly with others about my own feelings, and that the best things in life aren't *things* but people! (Beginning with grandchildren!)

My grandchildren have taught me in my midyears that it's important for them to have adults around who are crazy about kids. Grandchildren, and other little ones around us, need to know that there are adults who see them as priorities. They need adults to rub ministry shoulders with them. They need adults to listen, smile, laugh, cry, and play with them. They need adults who are just there—doing nothing but being friends.

And to those of you who are not grandfathers, no problem. There are probably little kids in your life who would enjoy spending time with you. The other day I stopped at a lemonade stand in the neighborhood. I think I was their first customer in over an hour. I asked them how much the lemonade was and they proudly showed me the sign that said, "5 cents a cup." I gave them a dollar and told them it was so nice of them to share a drink with me that they could keep the whole dollar as a tip. (Wow, big spender, huh?)

That was the best dollar I spent that day. The kids were so elated that someone took time for them. (Let alone helped them with their college fund!)

Last fall a young girl came to our door selling Girl Scout cookies. I did not recognize that she was one of our neighbors, so I told her that Hazel had already purchased gobs of cookies from other girls in green uniforms and that we weren't interested. With head down, she mumbled, "Thank you anyway," and walked away. I happened to watch her to see where she was going next and noticed her walk to her home, about four houses away. And then the guilt hit me. What was I doing? Turning away a neighbor's child just because we already had a freezer full of Snickerdoodles. I immediately put my hat and coat on and tramped over to her house. I apologized to her and explained that I had not recognized her, but I did want to help her in her crusade to sell the most cookies in Illinois. And it probably worked out better for her: I felt so guilty that I bought 10 boxes of cookies. What I learned that night is the importance of supporting and encouraging the young children around me. (By the way, if any of you want Girl Scout cookies, we still have a freezer full.)

In midlife, I've learned many lessons from children, and even a few from dogs and cats. Some health newsletters recently shared articles about what our cats and dogs can teach us. Here are a few of the lessons they list:

What our cats teach us:

1. Stretch often—with your whole body.

2. Remember to play.

3. Stay very clean.

4. Never lose your ability to be excited by something new.

5. When someone does something nice for you, remember to purr.

From *Health Promotion Practitioner,* P.O. Box 1335, Midland, MI. Used by permission.

What our dogs teach us:

1. Take plenty of walks and naps.

2. Don't think too much.

3. Never bite the hand that feeds you.

4. Bark when you feel like it.

5. Make friends with everyone in the neighborhood.

6. Make the people you love feel welcome when they come home.

7. Wag your tail a lot (smile and laugh).

8. Every now and then, stand out in the rain.

From *Making Wellness Fun Newsletter,* Leigh Ann Jasheway, 3247 Crocker Road, Eugene, OR. Used by permission.

One way to deal with the transitions during midlife is

to thank God for the little people, the cats and dogs, and other "things" that are all around us. Instead of getting locked into the seriousness of life, take time to enjoy, reflect, and keep in ministry range of grandchildren, other kids, and even cats and dogs.

And when a grandchild phones, or your dog needs to take a walk, or your neighbor wants to mow your lawn, consider seriously that this is another way that God keeps us sensitive to those special gifts around us.

FOR REFLECTION OR DISCUSSION

1. What have you learned from your grandchildren and/or other children around you?

2. Consider ways that you can spend time with younger people (and older people) around you. What can you do to help the generations connect more intentionally in your own family? in your neighborhood? in your congregation?

3. Share stories of what you have learned from grandchildren, cats, dogs, and other gifts around you.

4. Only the wisest and luckiest few of us maintain a child's heart as we mature. How can we keep childlike wonder in our hearts?

No Laughing Matter

The two scout leaders trudged up the trail along the inner rim of the Grand Canyon. A dozen or so exuberant scouts accompanied them. The boyish scouts were running back and forth on the trail, peering over the edge at every opportunity and thoroughly enjoying themselves. The younger scoutmaster was doing all right with the climb but his partner, a man of about 50, was in trouble. White-faced and panting, he was working painfully to get one foot in front of the other. Clearly, he was not going to be able to go on much longer. Finally, his foot caught on a stone and with no strength to stop himself, the scoutmaster fell into a heap, face down on the dusty trail. The scouts, as young people often do, found the fall quite hilarious. They broke out into raucous laughter. The scoutmaster struggled to a sitting position, fixed the gleeful scouts with his most withering stare and shouted, "This is no laughing matter!"

The pompous cleric swished out and took his place in front of the congregation. Just as he was about to begin the service, one of his notes fluttered from the book in his hands and settled on the floor in front of him. Portly and middle-aged, the parson did not relish having to bend to pick up the wayward note. But certain he would forget something if he did not, he bent over in a great dramatic bow to retrieve the lost information. As he bent, his toupee flipped up from the back and stood straight out from the top of his head. Erect again, the toupee remained at attention on his head, waving in the direction of the ceiling. Though some of the members of the congregation tried to catch their snicker, others could not help but break out into great gales of laughter. The parson retreated to the sacristy to regroup.

No laughing matter?

———

My brother (six years my junior) visited me at the office. One of the secretaries spotted us standing in the hall talking. "Oh," she said. "This must be your son." I must have scowled at her because the poor woman began to back away and make apologetic sounds. My brother found it quite funny. To me it was no laughing matter.

———

Indeed, as we grow into midlife, we may find many things that are to us no laughing matter. Increasing infirmity interferes with our ability to do what we want to do and is certainly no laughing matter. When we can't perform the way we used to, it is no laughing matter. When we make fools of ourselves, when others mark us as belonging to the "older generation," when we are ignored or discounted because we are "over the hill," it is certainly no laughing matter. In fact, the arrival of midlife itself is no laughing matter.

It is nearly impossible not to take ourselves too seriously as we grow older. At a minimum, it becomes more difficult to find the laughter and the joy in the events of the day. We tend to get into routines, take others for granted, see the darker side of things, feel we have "been there, done that." We may run around hanging black crepe paper on the dreams (which we would call illusions) of the younger people around us. We find ourselves saying "I told you so" a lot. We know from experience that much of life can be disappointing, so even in the best of circumstances we can find the gloomy side.

All of that can make midlife no laughing matter indeed. In fact, many of us midlifers seem to lose our ability to laugh. Oh, we probably laugh at parties when we are supposed to or when the laughter is lubricated by some alcohol. And we may laugh at an occasional movie or television program. We may even laugh at a cartoon or joke. But the day-to-day laughter that may have been a part of us when we were younger has escaped us.

A CRYING MATTER

The problem is that if our midlife foibles, follies, and failings are not laughing matters, they may become crying matters. We may find ourselves not only out of laughter but out of the joy of life altogether. We may find ourselves depressed—curmudgeons poking blaming fingers at the foolishness we see around us. We may be angry with others who seem to be having more fun than we are. We may become the kind of person that others—especially children—seek to avoid.

Perhaps that means it is time to cry. There is nothing wrong with a good cry—even for tough guys like us. It may be time to let out the sadness and grief we feel over the self that we have lost. It is all right to grieve over that loss. It is all right to remember our younger selves and feel great sadness for what used to be. It may be time to sit down and think about that loss and to weep real tears over it.

But then comes the time to dry the tears and get on with life. There is nothing wrong with sadness; we can learn from it. There is nothing wrong with crying—it can provide needed relief. But there is something wrong when we bury the sadness and the tears and let them become the force in us that robs us of the joy and laughter that midlife and beyond can bring.

Midlife can be a time of great joy. We are no longer required to spend most of our time trying to discover ourselves, look for a direction in life, question our decisions, scramble after our dreams. We don't have to spend all day in the office anymore. We don't have to construct great mountains of success for ourselves. We can be free to live. We can enjoy each day. We can ease into the demands of the day and find quiet places in the middle for reflection and renewal.

A MATTER OF LAUGHTER

Think of the people from your past, both middle-age and beyond, who stand out as stars in your memory. They may have been wise teachers, or parents or relatives, but very likely they were people of joy. We rarely remember those who walk through their midlife into their old age with a cloud of gloom about them. We rarely seek out those who approach the day with a drawn face and a narrowed vision. We avoid the complainers, the rainmakers, the pessimists. We seek out those who look at each day as an opportunity and the future as a challenge. We love to be with those who laugh.

Old Mazie (that's what they called her and what she called herself) certainly had a lot to complain about. She was in her late 80s and frail. She had arthritis in her feet, failing eyesight, heart trouble, and a dozen other maladies. Several of her children had died young and she had lost her husband 20 years before. She lived alone— but Mazie was almost never alone. People of all ages flocked around her. Why? For her wisdom? For her cleverness? For her ability to analyze the future or remember the past? Certainly none of those.

What drew people to Mazie was her laughter. In an instant, for almost no reason, Mazie would break into laughter. And no one could laugh like Mazie. She would rock herself and the rafters with the sheer volume of her joy. Her laughter was contagious. She would begin to laugh and invariably first the children and then the adults around her would laugh with her. She was a delight to have around because she brought what most church gatherings lacked—an expression of the sheer joy of being there, being together, and being alive. That was Mazie's gift. And Mazie was so popular that the children would wait for her outside the door of the church. People constantly dropped in on her at home. Mazie thought that life, though sometimes desperate and difficult, was a laughing matter indeed.

Not all of us can explode in gales of laughter at every occasion. We cannot all be sunny-of-face and constantly joyful. But we can decide, with God's help, to make our lives more laughing than crying matters.

THE BEST MEDICINE

Laughter has great healing power. Some years ago, a writer named Norman Cousins was afflicted by what was said to be a fatal disease. He set out to treat himself with laughter. He rented old comedy movies and made it a point to engage in "out loud" laughter for several hours a day. He claimed it cured him. It certainly turned his life around. Laughter is a way that our spirits are revitalized. Laughter is the work of God.

Certainly joy and laughter are gifts from God and the right responses to God's gracious gifts: Look up Luke 6:21 and Psalm 126:2. God promises that our sadness will be turned into joy (Psalm 30:11) and that along with nature (1 Chronicles 16:33) we will "sing for joy" because of what God has done for us (Psalm 71:23; Psalm 5:11). Jesus often refers to the joy of the believer as one of the features of faith. He says that we are to "ask … [in order that our] joy will be complete" (John 16:24). And St. Paul lists joy as a "fruit of the Spirit" (Galatians 5:22).

Of course, it is not easy to laugh when we feel depressed or to break into songs of joy when we feel lonely or anxious. Cultivating the gifts of joy and laughter takes attention and patience, but we can take steps toward finding life a "laughing matter":

1. Take time each day to step back from the events of the day and look for the humor. It is not funny to drop your coffee cup in the middle of a conversa-

tion. But looking back on it or telling someone else about it may help us find the laughter.

2. Take a second look. It may be easy to find fault, to see the failings in the dreams of others, to see the foolishness in some of the activity around us. It may be possible to break people's illusions and pour cold water on their plans. But taking a second look may enable us to catch some of their enthusiasm and join in the sheer joy of trying something that is an adventure even if it probably won't work.

3. Seek out others who know how to laugh. Age doesn't matter, but find those who know how to find joy and laughter in the world around them. Such people are rare treasures and we owe it to ourselves to be around them.

4. Don't take yourself too seriously. Certainly much of what we think and do is quite important. We have to attend to important tasks and make important contacts and keep important projects going. We have to see important people and attend important meetings. But all of that importance can give us the illusion that who we are and what we do is vital in God's plan for the world. Taking God's real, long-term perspective on what we busy ourselves with may help us keep a sense of humor about what we do and avoid believing that we are as important as we sometimes think we are. When we lose the ability to laugh at ourselves, we have lost most of our laughter.

5. Make it a point to laugh with someone else every day. That may take some planning and thought, but it should be possible to share laughter with another person—and shared laughter is joyful laughter.

6. Share the joy of others. St. Paul encourages us to "rejoice with those who rejoice" (Romans 12:15). Even when we cannot find much in our own lives to feel joyful about, we can share and celebrate happy events in the lives of others.

7. Focus on the positive. It is easy to be negative about most things. Seeing the positive in people and events takes practice, but it brings joy.

8. Spend time with children. Children bring us back to our center; they help us clarify what really is important in life. Children laugh from the heart and jump for joy at the little things in life. Even as we make our way through midlife we have important things to learn from children and to share with them. Best of all, children help us keep the child inside of us from getting buried.

9. Encounter God's awesome gifts in His creation. Stand on the edge of a canyon, look at the sunset across a lake, watch a wild animal, or take in the view from a mountaintop. As we hear creation praise God, the joy in our own souls is revitalized.

10. Spend time giving thanks. The complaints are easy. Self-pity comes almost automatically. We all seem to savor our troubles and trials. But the time we take

to consciously give thanks for the gifts and graces that fill our lives can help us keep the negatives in perspective and keep our spirit full of joy.

Indeed, midlife and the midlife muddle are not laughing matters. But we cannot allow the changes in our lives, the passing of time, or the graying of our heads to rob us of the joy and laughter that God would give us. We cannot be satisfied to turn inside ourselves, to become bitter and negative. To live in a cloud of self-pity and gloom is to deny what God has done for us and continues to give us.

Look up. Pay attention. See God's hand. Hear God speaking. The word is simple: In Christ, your life is a laughing matter indeed.

FOR REFLECTION OR DISCUSSION

1. Reflect on or share one really happy or joyful time in your life. What was it like? What joy do you find in remembering? How can remembering help you discover joy in your life today?

2. Look up some of the texts about joy and laughter listed above. What do they tell you about God's relationship to our joy? What does joy have to do with our faith? What good news do you find there?

3. Someone said, "Christians have the gift of joy in their hearts but most of them have not let their face know about it." True? Why or why not? True for you? How can you share your joy?

4. Write a letter to someone you know who has lost the gift of joy and laughter in life. What can you say?

What can you share? How does the letter apply to you as well?

A RESURRECTION ACTION

Write down a plan for yourself that will help you discover or rediscover some of the joy and happiness in your life. Decide what you will do, how you will do it, and with whom you will share the quest. Carry through on your plan and then reevaluate. How can finding and sharing joy continue to be an important part of your life?

FOUR

Matters of Midlife and the Spiritual Journey

The Way

A DAY OF RE-CREATION

The phone had rung once too often. The demands on my time got to be too much. The voices in my ear seemed constant. I didn't even have time to think. I longed for some time alone to reflect, to sort things out. I longed for a time of renewal when I could get my head together, do some planning, and try to make some sense out of the rush of days.

I chose a day a couple weeks away and guarded it jealously. That was going to be my renewal day—my day of re-creation, my day to myself.

On that day, I set out early. I drove to a wooded area not too far from home. (I didn't want to spend the day in the car.) I found the end of the trail I had been told was there and started walking.

The day was beautiful. The sun cut through the trees and spotted the path. The clouds were in the sky, the birds in the trees, the wind brushed gently through the branches around me. The peace I sought seemed near, perhaps just around the next bend. Perhaps a little farther up the trail.

The trail through the woods started out wide and well maintained. But before long I seemed to be on a trail that was almost unused. Dried leaves covered the path and bushes and branches invaded my walking space.

At first my time of re-creation had been near perfect. I had time to think as I walked along, time to reflect, recount, remember. I had time to ask questions of myself that had long been set aside: Am I getting where I wanted to be? Is my life going somewhere? Are my relationships working? Do I want to keep going this way with my career? Does my life have value? Does it offer any reward to me? If I died tomorrow, would I feel that my time on this earth had been worth anything? Would I leave any mark? Would anyone care if I was gone?

On the wide path early in the day the questions were comfortable, but as the path narrowed and the woods darkened, so did my thoughts. I found worries and disappointments pulling at me: Why was I not where I wanted to be? Why was I so often driven to do things I didn't really want to do? Why was I so often with people I didn't really want to be with? Did my life make a difference? If so, to whom? Who really cared? Was there any reward?

The path seemed to disappear altogether. I was stumbling through heavy underbrush and there seemed to be no direction to my travel. Had I lost the path? Where did I make the wrong turn? Where did I go wrong? Where was I headed? Was I going back the way I came? Did it make sense to keep going ahead? What direction was I supposed to go?

Briars pulled at my pants and roots trapped my feet as I tried to walk. Several times I fell. Each time I got up I seemed to be less sure of what to do next.

And my reflection seemed to be stumbling too. Where was I going with my life? Did it matter? Did I have any direction at all? I started out to do something with my life, to accomplish something, to spend time so that it would be of value to someone. What happened?

Was I really going backwards, getting nowhere for all my work, the time, and frustration of my daily living? Did I not find myself being grabbed at by problems that didn't really have much to do with what I wanted to get done? Why was my life cluttered with demands and tasks and claims on me that just confused things more?

And what about those times I fell—the mistakes I made, the times I chose the wrong path, the times I just plain messed up? Who was there to pick me up? Who understood? Who cared?

Now, at the midpoint of my life, I sometimes felt like I was on a trail going nowhere and that no one cared whether I made it. I felt like I did not know where I was supposed to be going, whether I had a purpose. I felt lost.

At that point on my day of re-creation, I found myself sitting under a tree, praying. I was praying partly that I would find my way out of the woods and back to the trail that would take me to my car and home. But even more, I was praying that God would find me on my journey through life and help me get back to a trail that was right for me and that would eventually get me home.

THE NARROWING PATH

We are told that in midlife, many men experience a spiritual desert. God seems far away, the work of daily living seems to take all waking time. There's little time for spiritual renewal, for quiet time to commune with God. There's little opportunity to search through the stillness and come to terms with the passing of the days. There's just no time. There are tasks to be done. There is work to be done. There are jobs waiting. There are people depending on us. Money has to be saved for college for the kids and for retirement. People around us are getting ahead and we seem to be slipping back. Our ability to do the "right" thing is tested constantly against the need to do the expedient thing.

If life is a spiritual journey, then midlife is the most difficult, lonely, and confusing part of the journey. Midlife is the time when the spiritual journey can become a difficult wandering along an obscure path, through brambles and briars, toward an unclear goal. Midlife can lead us to a place where we feel spiritually lost.

BRIGHT BEGINNINGS

It's strange that it happens that way. Many of us started out on a spiritual path that was clear and well maintained. We had a sense of God's presence in our lives as we came out of our youth. We were aware that God had set a path before us that would allow us to make not only a living, but a life that had meaning and purpose.

Many of us came into our careers with an intention to make a contribution, to go about our work in such a way that it would be of value to God and others. We intended to follow the way that God would have us go, to live a life that would have a measure of service in it, that would touch others and give us a sense of accomplishment. We may have told ourselves that we were not so much interested in "making it big" or "getting rich"; we really wanted to make our life into something that mattered, that we could be proud of.

Many of us had a sense of being on a broad and inviting spiritual journey as we began our careers and our marriages. But for some of us, the years have narrowed the path. So many things seem to get in the way of our good intentions. The demands on our time and on the money we could earn can be so much more pressing than we expected. The rewards for time spent in service can be so much less than we expected. No one seems to be grateful when we give of our time. No one seems to care if we do volunteer work or not.

And our sense of being close to God and to His will for us may have faded as well. In reality, we sometimes make compromises with our conscience and with our perception of God's will as we make our way up the career ladder. There seem to be few rewards for those who hold too tightly to "doing the right thing." Those who are able to present false images of themselves, to blow their own horns (often at the expense of others), those who can cut corners and get things done despite the cost seem to be respected and to get ahead. It is not often that talent wins out. Instead, those who know how to work the angles, force themselves in—even in places where they are not wanted—are the ones who get ahead. It is lonely to sit on a career plateau and have only our integrity for company.

The path narrows then. The spiritual journey darkens. The hand of God in our life seems absent. The hopes and dreams we started with become disappointment and frustration.

SOME MIDLIFE JOURNEYERS

Let's look at some of these midlife men and ask ourselves: Do I see myself in them?

Perry the President. Perry has it made. He's built his bank account and his two-story house to impressive size. He's respected in the community. He has a hand in lots of deals. Sometimes Perry has to look the other way when his friends or associates cut the corners of the law to get the best investment or to get ahead of the competition. Perry wants for nothing but time. He lacks nothing but inner peace. Perry looks in the mirror in the morning and is satisfied with his accomplishments. But Perry dares not look in the mirror too long. There in his eyes, Perry does not see the idealistic youth he once knew. There, in that place where Perry kept his hopes and dreams, he finds emptiness.

Walter the Workman. Walter puts in lots of time at his job. He goes in early and stays late. He says that he has to to keep up. It used to be easier to keep up, but now the younger people are pressing him from behind. Walter attended his son's high school graduation just last week. He was really proud. His son graduated fifth in his class. But nagging questions kept at Walter all through the ceremony: When did I have time to really get to know my son? When did we spend time together? When did we get to know that we like each other? How did that time slip away?

Ervin the Excellent. Ervin has his doctorate now. He worked toward it for years. He's a respected teacher and scholar. His work is often published and many people seem to be impressed with his accomplishments. He's at the top of his profession. He's often listed among the most respected in his field. But his wife doesn't know him very well anymore, and he has few friends. Almost no one has time for him. Ervin works a lot, but no one seems to be there when he just wants to have a good time.

Stan the Striver. Stan has worked for the same company for 20 years. He's an important part of the operation. He knows how things work in the company and is often asked questions by the younger people. But Stan is still doing about what he did when he started with the company. Oh, he's got a slightly larger office now. And over the years, he's supervised quite a few of the people who work for the company. But Stan, for all his striving, seems to be at a dead end. Stan keeps asking himself: Will I have to do this same job for 20 more years? Stan doesn't like the question, and he's found that a couple of drinks with the boys after work softens the answer.

Frank the Friendly. Frank loves to be around people. His job lets him work with people and he enjoys the interaction. He spends a lot of time with his friends at bars and events. He's even joined several clubs to meet other people with similar interests. But Frank has lived through two divorces and now lives alone. His child support and alimony payments keep him nearly broke and he longs to be able to go out more. For some reason, despite Frank's friendliness, he can't seem to get close to others—even the women he married. When Frank looks in the mirror, he sees loneliness.

Of course, the men here represent only a few of those who come into midlife and find the path narrowing. We can probably all see part of ourselves in these men and can tell many similar stories. But the real question is not why is the spiritual path becoming more difficult? The real question is what are we going to do about it?

FINDING THE PATH AGAIN

It is not likely that we can blunder through midlife and suddenly discover the bright path of spiritual wellness again. It is not likely that we will wake up some morning and suddenly find ourselves satisfied with our lives, happy in our careers, content in our relationships, and clear about our brightening future. Those instant spiritual renewals happen, but they are pretty rare and sometimes quite fleeting.

If we want to revitalize our spiritual life and get back on the path of spiritual health, we have to invite God into the process, pay attention to the renewal, and be willing to invest time in getting back on track.

The same Jesus who said, "My yoke is easy and My burden is light," (Matthew 11:30) also said, "If anyone would come after Me, he must deny himself and take up his cross and follow Me" (Matthew 16:24). He also said "narrow" is the way that leads to life (Luke 13:24).

Certainly we can continue to muddle our way through. We can get so busy with *making* a living that we won't have to *do* much living. We can concentrate so hard on daily tasks that we will hardly notice the days going by. We can invest so much of our energy into blundering ahead that we won't even notice the emptiness that gnaws at us when we can't block out the thoughts anymore.

FALSE SOLUTIONS

Many people are making a great deal of money selling midlifers self-help courses or programs that are supposed to make life successful and happy, and leave the users of the programs fulfilled. These self-made solutions come in a variety of forms. Some folks offer seminars that are supposed to revitalize life. Others publish books. Some offer one-on-one counseling. Others invite people into support groups.

And in reality, there is probably nothing terribly harmful about any of these. It may make our life better if we get into a program that gives us a clearer picture of ourselves and our future. We may find help in the story of someone who has successfully overcome their midlife crisis. And we might be enriched by counseling or support relationships with others who are dealing with midlife issues.

But none of these offers a permanent (dare we say eternal) solution to the problem of our spiritual emptiness. None of them can give us tools to overcome the basic problem in ourselves. In truth, in the face of the confusion and conflicting demands of midlife, we are not equipped to make ourselves better. We have no inner tricks that can fill the emptiness in the center of ourselves.

The hole in the middle of life can only be filled from the outside—by the Spirit of God who, by the Gospel, continues to call us, enlighten us, renew us, and move us toward wholeness. The failures and frustrations that can be so much a part of midlife can only be removed by the eternal gift of God's forgiveness in Jesus Christ.

THE BRIGHTENING PATH

When I was on that walk in the woods, I found myself still wandering as the sun began to set. I still had no real clue as to where I was or which way was out. I could find no path in the woods that made any sense to me. But then suddenly, almost like a miracle, I looked through the trees and saw the parking lot where I had left my car. It was, I guess, a minor miracle. I certainly didn't have the skill to get back to my car by myself. I found no path through the woods to help me. But suddenly I was there. Almost as if someone had guided me. And when I got in my car and started for home, I felt grateful—not just for being able to get back out again, but for the experience of the day.

The most important thing I learned that day was that given the time in my life, my talents and abilities, the time I had left, and the inner strength I was able to muster, I could not do it by myself. Left on my own, I would continue to wonder and wander and stumble. I would continue to give the illusion that I know where I am going when I am really lost. I came to know even more clearly that if my life is going to be valuable and satisfying, it will be by the grace of God.

And by God's grace, I walk a brighter path now. Not perfect, mind you. I don't always know what I am up to. I don't always have satisfying answers to the questions that too often nag me. I am not always sure I am living out God's will or heading in God's way. But I'm doing better.

Things are better because I know that I have to make time to listen for the Spirit every day—and not just on a set-aside day when I can take a walk in the woods. I know that I have the privilege of waking each day knowing that I am renewed by the gift of God's forgiveness in Jesus Christ. I know that every day I am able to go on because the Spirit dwells in me and the Savior is with me.

That knowledge sustains me along the path to the fulfillment that God has in store for me. And I know as I journey:

> *The LORD is my shepherd,*
>> *(He continues to guide me, even when I stray.)*
>
> *I shall not be in want. (I will not be left orphaned.)*
>
> *He makes me lie down in green pastures,*
> *He leads me beside quiet waters,*
>> *(Even when I don't want to take the time for it.)*

He restores my soul. *(Even when I don't deserve it.)*

He guides me in paths of righteousness for His
  name's sake. *(Certainly not for mine.)*

Even though I walk through the valley of the shadow
  of death, *(and along the most obscure paths)*

I will fear no evil,
  (I've been there before—and never alone.)

for You are with me; ...
  (When I realize it and when I don't.)

Surely goodness and love will follow me
  (like a miracle)

all the days of my life, *(through midlife and beyond)*

and I will dwell in the house of the Lord *forever.*
  (Where else can I belong?)

Psalm 23

THE WAY OF THE CROSS/
THE WAY OF THE OPEN TOMB

It is interesting to note that in the early centuries, Christianity was known as "The Way." Those who were followers of Christ—and even those on the outside— recognized that being a disciple of Jesus was not just knowing that He existed or agreeing with His teachings. To be a follower of Jesus meant that the disciple was willing to live "the way" Jesus lived.

Some think that following Jesus is an escape. They think it is a way to avoid the hardships and difficulties of life. They want to believe it is a way to strike a bargain with God so He will give them good gifts and protection from the pains of life.

It is not so. Jesus invites us to follow Him. He invites us to make the way that He walked through the world *our* path. He promises abundance, peace, reward, and much more as we follow Him.

But the way we are invited to follow is still the way of the cross. It is the way of sacrifice and sometimes of sorrow. It is the way that much of the world considers foolishness. It is a way that demands much and offers little of the rewards of this earth.

"Do not be surprised," Jesus said, "if the world hates you" (1 John 3:13). Certainly, if they do not hate us, they do not understand us. Why would you take talents and spend them following the Savior? Why would you take the things you have acquired and give them away? Why would you want to spend time with the undeserving? Why would you want to be servant of all?

That kind of living, the world might say, could get you in trouble. In fact, it could get you crucified.

And yet we follow. Not because we believe the way Jesus calls us to walk is easy. Not because we believe we will avoid the hurts and trials of life. Not even because we believe we will avoid the cross that way. We follow because the way is guaranteed. Jesus has walked the way already. The path is clear and the way is sure. We cannot be driven, enticed, threatened, forced, or coerced from the path of Jesus.

And we know this: The way is not only the way of the cross but the way of the open tomb. Because we have "already died with Christ," we already enjoy the resurrection. We stand in the face of the world and affirm that no ending, no dead end, no stopping place, no barrier, no hidden path, no darkened woods, no desert valley, not even death itself can stop us from "dwelling in the house of the Lord," now and eternally.

In that promise we walk the way—God's promising way.

FOR REFLECTION OR DISCUSSION

1. Describe your spiritual journey. Take a large piece of paper and draw a line representing your years. Let the line move up to show the good times. Use a line that dips into a valley to show the bad times. Then go back and note the important events happening along that lifeline. Note some of the significant people.

   • Reflect on your spiritual journey. How was God involved in all the events and relationships? What kind of path can you discover at various times along the way?

   • Give your journey a title. What might the story of that journey be called? How would you share that journey story with someone else?

   • Project the line of your journey into the future. Indicate where you would like the journey to go. Where do you think it will go? What events do you look forward to? What relationships? What good times? How will God be involved in that future?

2. Read in your Bible about of the following journeys:

Abraham: Genesis 12:1–9

Jacob: Genesis 28

Israel: Exodus 40:34–38

Elijah: 1 Kings 19

The man on the way to Jericho: Luke 10:29–37

The "sent out" disciples: Matthew 10:5–23

Jesus' family: Luke 2:41–52

Paul: Acts 21.

What can we learn about our spiritual journeys from these accounts? What assurance is God giving us? What can we depend on? How are we equipped to journey?

3. Meet with another person who has completed most of his successful spiritual journey. What can you discover about how to journey from your conversation? What do faith, hope, and purpose have to do with that journey? What can you learn from this leader in the faith?

A RESURRECTION ACTION

Gather with two or three other midlife journeyers. Share some stories of your journeys. What similarities and differences do you see? What encouragement can you offer to one another?

Make a commitment to meet together regularly (weekly) for several months. Talk about your hopes for your journey into the future. Read and study Scripture together. Set out specific tasks or challenges that you intend to undertake and report the results to one another. Continue your group as it is helpful to you.

The Hopes and Fears of All the Years

I never realized until now that the hymn "O Little Town of Bethlehem" is a great resource for us middle-aged men. Just listen to some of the words again: "The hopes and fears of all the years are met in Thee tonight." What a great theme for middle-age!

Our hopes for the future and our fears of the past come together in Christ. And that's not just some fluffy line from a Christmas hymn—that's a reality that the Lord gives to us each day.

I'm continually amazed at the number of times the phrase "Don't be afraid" is used in the Scriptures. Take your hopes and fears into the Scriptures and listen again to the Lord's comforting words, "Don't be afraid!" The angels bring those words of affirmation to the shepherds on that first Christmas Eve; the women at the Easter tomb hear it; Zechariah hears it as recorded in Luke 1:13; Paul uses it to comfort himself and his followers. And on and on.

"Don't be afraid" is not a command from the Lord, but an affirmation of His presence among us. It's like the feeling a little child has when a lightning storm strikes and he crawls into bed with Mom and Dad. As he snuggles under the covers with the warmth of his parents around him, he hears from them the soft, comforting words, "Don't be afraid—I am here."

The one fact that moves me from my shadows of the past into my hopes for the future is that the Lord continues to be with me each day. Though we "walk through the valley of the shadow of death," we fear no evil because God is with us. To be truthful, I still do fear evil and, as a matter of fact, I would rather not walk through the valley of the shadow of death—if anything, I'd like to at least run through it. But the comfort I have and the assurance we all have is that the Lord is there to comfort and guide us, even when we don't feel or act or look like it.

Part of our problem of dealing with the shadows of our past is that too many of us have learned to hide our past and not talk about our feelings. Remember that old ditty, "Whenever I feel afraid, I hold my head erect and whistle a happy tune so no one will suspect I'm afraid!" How sad! We do not need to hide our fears and make believe that everything is going well. That's part of our problem. If we feel like singing at all, perhaps we should sing, loudly and clearly, "Whenever I feel afraid, I hold my head erect and shout I'M AFRAID!"

The only way we are able to deal with our past and move into the future with hope is to realize that all our hopes and fears really *are* "met in Thee tonight." It's at the intersection of the cross and the empty tomb that the shadows can fade and the hopes can be dreamed. The hopes and fears of all our years will continue to be with us, you can count on that. But we can also count on the fact that these hopes and fears have already been handled by the Lord through His death and resurrection. And that's why we can boldly proclaim to ourselves and to those around us, "Hey, no need to be afraid— Christ is with us!"

REMEMBERED

In a discussion group not so long ago the topic centered around what each of us wanted to be remembered for. One quick response came from a 45-year-old who said, "I really don't care, I just want to be remembered." And that's a mouthful. Each of us no doubt wants to leave a mark—our legacy—in life. It may be that none of us will change the world drastically, but we can have positive effects in significant and insignificant ways as we relate with the people around us. And, in a sense, that does make a difference in this world. Mother Theresa (certainly past her midlife years at this writing) frequently answers the question "Are you making any real difference in the world?" by quietly saying, "I'm not sure, but I do know I'm making a significant difference in the lives of individuals."

So what's the 45-year-old who wants to be remembered to do? He could play the game "Write Your Own Epitaph." Have you ever played it? What would you want your tombstone to say to the next generation? Few of us would have it say, "I wish I would have spent more time in the office." How do you want to be remembered?

FOR REFLECTION OR DISCUSSION

1. Talk with other people about what might be put on your tombstone by your wife, best friend, family members, co-workers.

2. Share some of your "shadows" of the past with someone close to you.

3. Share some of your hopes and dreams with someone close to you. Ask that person to share his or her hopes and dreams also.

4. What piece of hope can you give to someone today? Watch for the opportunities.

FIVE

Matters of Success and Failure

The Mountain

Once, on a whim or a dare, we climbed a mountain—
my son and I. He was only 12 or so. We were on a
fishing trip, somewhere in southern Missouri. There was
a mountain near where we were camped, an Ozark mountain pushing its head toward the clouds. On that trip the
mountain became our friend. It covered the afternoon
sun and made the fish turn to evening feeding earlier as
the shadow of the mountain crept across the lake.

"Let's climb it, Dad." Ted said. His enthusiasm
caught me.

"Okay," I heard myself saying. "Let's give it a try."

We set off in the morning with a canteen of water,
some Granola bars, and a lot of hope. The mountain was
a lot farther off than we expected. It was nearly noon by

75

the time we reached the trail at the foot of the mountain that led up the slope. The sign said: "CAUTION: Seven mile trail. Steep and rocky. For advanced climbers." We didn't talk about the sign. We just kept walking.

It was nearing evening and we were sliding back on the loose gravel on yet another particularly tricky slope. My hands were scratched and bleeding from grabbing at branches and bushes to pull myself up again and again. Ted's pants were torn and his tennis shoes sported new vents in several places.

We sat under a tree. The sun was already hiding behind the mountain.

"We can make it, Dad," he said. "We can do it. Can't we?"

Well, could we? I knew that even if we started back right then, it would be dark by the time we got back to camp. And then what about the living things in the woods we could not see and could not control? And what if I fell and broke a bone? What could he do? What if he fell and really hurt himself? Where would I get help?

"We have to turn back," I said. Ted's face fell. "We're just not equipped to make this climb. We should have started earlier. And we didn't know we needed real climbing shoes and gloves, not to mention ropes."

"But, Dad."

"Listen. I know you're disappointed, but we can come back some other day. We'll bring the right clothing and equipment. We'll wait until fall when it's cooler. We'll make sure we have enough food and water. Then we'll run up this old mountain just like it wasn't there."

But we never did.

THE OTHER MOUNTAIN

Twenty or more years ago, I set out on another mountain. But this mountain was not approached on a whim. It was a part of my plan.

The top of that mountain was the place I planned to be by now. By this time of my life, I thought, I would know what the top of the mountain looked like, what it felt like, what it could give me. When I reached the top of my mountain, I could look down at others still struggling to get there; I could hold my head up and get the respect—even the applause—of many who had seen me climb. I could enjoy the view from the top of my mountain of success. I would have made it to where I wanted to be, where I had striven to be. There at the top, I could feel good about what I had done, enjoy what I had worked for. I could say I had made it.

But the climb over the years has been more difficult than I expected. Too often I found myself in slippery spots—places where the footing was not sure, places I had to make decisions about which way to turn. I have grabbed and pulled and struggled to get where I am now. I have passed a few other climbers on the way but been passed by many more.

Many times I have found myself sitting under a tree, resting on what I have accomplished, unable or unwilling to set out for the next level. Why? I'm not lazy. I've never been afraid of work. Is it the chance that I won't be able to make it that holds me back? Is it my fear of failure that keeps me from trying? Is it my need to protect myself from pain that keeps me sitting under a tree instead of getting out on the trail?

Now, at midlife, I find myself again under a sheltering tree. "We can still make it to the top," my heart says to me with the voice of the child that still lives somewhere in me. "We can do it."

But the sun is going down. The days are shorter. The time is slipping away. I don't have the strength I used to have. The younger, talented ones move so much more quickly than I do. The way gets steeper up ahead. How much longer can I drive forward before the night comes?

THE MOUNTAINTOP THAT CANNOT BE

Just the other day I went climbing with my son again. He's grown now—a young man—strong, determined. He wears the proper climbing equipment. He knows how to move up a trail. He waited for me as we made our way on the first mile of the uphill trail not far from our home. He was patient with me as I tried to keep up. After a while he said, "Dad, why don't you just wait here, and I'll go the rest of the way. I'll be back in a couple hours. You can fish over there or something till I get back." And he was gone.

I know now that I will never make the top of the mountain. It's too far and it's too late. Some of my dreams are on the top of the mountain. I won't ever get there to capture them. I will never stand out above all who climbed with me, never receive their applause, never catch the view of the horizon I thought I needed. Never …

Did God play a trick on me? Did God give me the vision to look to the top of the mountain and only enough talent and strength to reach halfway? Did God create in me a desire to achieve greatness and only give me the ability to achieve mediocrity? Did God set me up for failure, give me hopes and dreams that could never be? Did God mean for me to spend the rest of my life moving back down the hill I thought I could climb, back down past those still climbing, back down to the valley where I started, where I had nothing and was nothing?

Or, did I do it all myself?

The sense of failure and disappointment that I felt as my son and I headed back down the mountain we could not climb comes easily to me now, at this time in my life, when I look at my own mountain of dreams that I could not climb.

OF BROKEN DREAMS

The experts tell us that one of the things we have to do at midlife is become comfortable with where we are. We are supposed to come to terms with where we will likely end our lives. We are supposed to put away the dreams that we will never fulfill. Midlife is a time of bumping up against reality. It can be a time of disappointment, even despair.

Some of the panic we see in the eyes of others who have reached midlife may be their inability to accept that the mountain they have set out to climb is too high for them. It may be the realization that they will never "have it made." That realization can cause them to do strange and seemingly destructive things. They suddenly change careers, or life companions, or move to another place. Or, they drift into a dependence on alcohol, or pursue some hobby with such a vengeance that it threatens to destroy their home and work life.

It is difficult to quit before one reaches the top of the mountain. It's easy to blame God for the failure—for seeming to give us the desire and not the ability. It's easy to turn our anger on God who did not, it seems, give us the same chances as others, open the same doors for us. It's easy to drift into a bitterness that darkens our life. It's easy to become depressed and fall even farther behind.

We seem to operate with the illusion that one of God's promises is success. We search the Bible for a passage that says: "If you work real hard, God will give you what you deserve." Or maybe what we think we deserve. It is a tempting illusion.

CLIMBING THE WRONG PROMISE

God *does* promise success and happiness and peace as we live out our relationships with Jesus Christ and one another. But those gifts don't have much to do with striving, gaining, grasping, getting, or achieving. They have to do with the opposite: giving and giving up, accepting and opening, denying, and carrying crosses. God's success has to do with finding our life by losing it (Matthew 10:39). Hard words, hard truths for that part of us that still wants to make it to the top of the mountain.

Jesus talked often about the perils of the rich. He warned about the farmer with the bigger barns that did him no good (Luke 12:16–21). He told the rich young man, "Sell your possessions and give to the poor" (Matthew 19:21). He told His disciples, "If anyone would come after Me, he must deny himself and take up his cross and follow Me" (Mark 8:34). And He clarifies the message in Matthew 16:26: "What good will it be for a man if he gains the whole world, yet forfeits his soul?"

The mountain that we are called to climb is not the mountain of our dreams but God's mountain. It may be a mountain of suffering for the sake of another, or the mountain of giving until we seem to have nothing for ourselves. It may be the mountain of serving until we seem to be taken for granted by those being served. All of those mountains can be set before us as God calls us to climb them.

But there is a difference between God's mountains and the ones we create for ourselves. Every mountain that God sets before us does not merely promise us success, it guarantees us success. Jesus climbed the mountain already. We don't even have to find the trail. The footsteps to follow are there. Even the strength to put one spiritual foot in front of another is given to us as a gift. It is called living in the promise.

A MODEL MOUNTAIN CLIMBER

Want to climb a better mountain? Look at Smitty.

Smitty was the self-appointed town character in the small town where we lived when we were first married. Smitty was unforgettable. He looked like a toothless Santa Claus in scrounged clothing. By any standard measure of success, he was an abject failure. He owned no property, no car, paid no taxes, had no bank account. His "fix it shop" business collected small appliances he never got around to fixing. He wandered the town "visiting"— as he put it—with everyone. In that self-important, rushed, and sometimes frantic little town, Smitty always had time: to watch a store for a haggard owner, to push a baby carriage for a frazzled mother, to pick flowers with the children, and to visit with the abandoned ones who sat on the courthouse benches.

Smitty glowed with the joy of life. He had been the town drunk. Health broken by the time he was 40, he'd lost everything that people value. Alone and in a gutter, as he told the story, God found him and put him on his feet again. He said he was living on God's time—not his own. He had no time for gaining and getting and owning—only for giving and living and laughing and doing—and for sharing the story of "my Savior's" love, as he said it.

Smitty was certainly the town character. But among the earnest and graceless strugglers up the mountain of success in that town (including a self-consciously dedicated young pastor) Smitty floated like an overweight, disorganized, disreputable, grace-filled, graceful spirit. And he taught us all how to live.

Sometimes in my imagination I see us standing before Christ's throne of judgment.

"And what have you done with the talents and abilities, the opportunities and time that you have been given?" the Lord asks me.

"Well, I made it halfway up the mountain of my dreams. I accumulated enough to be comfortable. I tried to be fair in my dealings and not too selfish in my taking. I made it farther than some others who grew up with me and some people even call me a success," I say.

Then Smitty steps up. "Well, Lord," he says with a smile on his face. "I never had much, never needed much, never did much that would be called an accomplishment. I took what You gave me and gave it away to others who needed it more than I."

And then I see the Lord smile. "Well done, good and faithful servant ..." And He's not talking to me.

Finally, this truth remains. The mountain of my success is an illusion, a creation of my need. The sadness is not that I have struggled and only made it halfway, but that I have struggled at all.

GOD HAS ANOTHER JOURNEY IN MIND FOR US

We are called to be on a pilgrim journey—walking along a road of His choosing, carrying the equipment of His Good News, meeting and greeting, walking with and helping those who walk the way with us.

But this we can know more surely than anything else: If it is true that "to live is Christ and to die is gain" (Philippians 1:21) then it's not too late for us to find the way and walk the path that God sets out before us.

The path will not reach the top of the mountain of our dreams. It will not gain us attention or applause. It will not make our lives comfortable or put money in the bank. It may instead lead to rejection, pain, and discouragement.

But it is the way that God has set out for us. It is the

way of purpose and promise.

And with the joy of those who no longer have to scramble up impossible mountains of our own making and our own frustration, we walk in the footsteps of those like Smitty and Jesus. We walk in step with the promise of God and with one another.

FOR REFLECTION OR DISCUSSION

1. What does your mountain of success look like? What draws or drives you toward the top? How do you feel about making or not making it to the top of the mountain of your dreams? What does God have to do with your mountain?

2. Look up and read through the passages listed in this section. What is Jesus telling you in those passages? To what kind of life is He calling you? What difference in your life would it make if the Spirit would help you follow His call?

3. Our life on this earth has been compared to a battle, a journey, a climb, a race, a time of testing. Which of those seems most like your understanding of life? How do others fit into your understanding of life?

4. Think about or describe one person you would consider a success. What is that person like? What values does he or she show? Which of his or her qualities would you like to imitate? How would the world assess that person? Where does that person find happiness?

A RESURRECTION ACTION

Take time to assess where you are in your "climb" through life. Talk to someone else about it. How do you feel about the years you have spent? What have you gained? If you could change one thing about your life right now, what would it be? Say a prayer and ask for the Spirit's power to begin that change, a little at a time.

Who Needs Friends? We Do!

Journeying through the predictable and necessary midlife crisis, men begin to examine the lack of meaning in acquiring material things and instead of asking what, how, or when, we start to ask why. Friends become a very important part of this journey.

How many close friends do you have? How many do you need? How many of us have played our lives so close to the vest that we find ourselves having to admit, "I don't think I have any close friends." The truth is we need friendship—literally. Many reports show that warm social ties and secure relationships can boost immune functions, improve the quality of life, lower the risk of cancer and other physical and mental health conditions at any age. We *need* friends.

And friendship is a gift from God. One of the saddest verses of Scripture is John 20:24: "Thomas ... was not with the disciples when Jesus came." Thomas missed out on so much! Because he disconnected himself from his friends, he was not there for a miraculous moment in the life of the disciples: Jesus' appearance after the resurrection. The other disciples, though fearful and unsure, at least had each other to form their "holy huddle."

Friends are ways that God supports us with His presence in other people. We need each other so very much, especially in times when we may not think we need each other. As Jethro said to Moses when he was trying to do everything by himself and not asking for help from his friends, "What you are doing is not good. You and these people who come to you will only wear yourselves out. The work is too heavy for you; you cannot handle it alone" (Exodus 18:17). What a relief! We don't need to handle midlife alone—we have our friends (God's gifts to us) and our Friend, Jesus.

MIDLIFE LONERS

Recent research continues to show that, in general, men do not give one another affection. Men do not talk to one another about intimate things. Men do not nurture one another. Men do not have complete or whole relationships. There is often a lack of genuine immediate friendships among men, not to speak of lifelong friendships. Leonard Sweet, in his book *The Jesus Prescription for a Healthy Life,* (Abingdon Press, 1996) says it this way:

> *What does it profit, Jesus said, if you gain the whole world, and lose your soul?*

What does it profit, if you gain the whole world, and spend your life in an office?

What does it profit, if you gain the whole world, and spend your days on a golf course?

What does it profit, if you gain the whole world, and never know your children?

What does it profit, if you gain the whole world, and never have a best friend?

What does it profit, if you gain the whole world, and can't keep the joy, much less "let a joy keep you"?

What does it profit, if you gain the whole world, and never consider the lilies, much less smell the roses?

What does it profit, if you gain the whole world, and lose your soul?

Sweet also draws a correlation between loneliness and mental illness. He points out that some people sojourn at mental health centers because at points of crisis in their lives, they were alone. In contrast, the Amish have a community spirit so strong that they ask one question of any proposed change: "What will this do to our community?" And studies show that they are only one-fifth as vulnerable to depression as other Americans. What marvelous gifts community and friendships are!

A connected life is not only a contented life, it is also a healthy life. A network of healthy relationships is one of the best vaccines for depression, disease, and even death. Healthy friendships can ease the burden of midlife.

THE TITUS TOUCH

God's plan for healing in our lives comes by what some have called *The Titus Touch.* "But God, who comforts the downcast, comforted us by the coming of Titus" (2 Corinthians 7:6). Titus was Paul's chosen traveling companion and trusted co-worker. Paul sensed the importance of friendship and allowed Titus to use his gifts of health and healing. *The Titus Touch*—not a bad way to think about friendship and the power of the Lord in our lives!

Current studies characterize what happens when a middle-aged man is caught in the "muddle" of life:

1. He keeps things that bother him to himself.

2. He fears letting people know him.

3. He denies that unpleasant things are happening.

4. He has difficulty interacting with his parents, spouse, and kids.

5. He has a strong fear of criticism.

6. He becomes angry.

7. He can't express his feelings.

8. He disproportionately fears failure.

9. He desperately wants his life to be better, but doesn't know how to change it.

Can you identify with any of these characteristics? I certainly can. And the point is not so much that we can identify, but what we can do to deal with these situations positively. The whole message of midlife is that the Lord is providing us opportunities to change some of our directions in life, review our values, and move into new stages of development in positive and progressive ways.

MAKING A DIFFERENCE

We men in the middle have a great opportunity to make a difference in our own lives and in the lives of people around us. Instead of regretting and wishing that we could start over, we can decide right now to forget the past and begin to work at making the days ahead more fruitful, productive, and pleasing to the Lord. He wipes away the past and empowers us to move into the future.

Psalm 90 is a good resource for reflecting on our past, present, and future. First, the psalmist reminds us that the Lord has been our "dwelling place throughout all generations" (v. 1). Verse 5 reminds us that each day is new with blessings from the Lord. And verse 10: "The length of our days is seventy years—or eighty, if we have the strength; yet their span is but trouble and sorrow, for they quickly pass, and we fly away."

And then the psalmist pleads with the Lord to "satisfy us in the morning with Your unfailing love, that we may sing for joy and be glad all our days" (v. 14). This joy in the Lord is never a solo act. God has put us in communities to share our sorrows and our joys from morning to evening. No one is an island—we're all connected

with the waters of Baptism. Our friendship with the Lord
and with those around us is centered on the fact that the
Lord came to live, suffer, die, and rise for each of us. Our
Baptism marks us as a community of faith, the commu-
nion of saints.

A friend of mine likes to compare the church, the
body of Christ, with mountain climbers. He says the only
reason mountain climbers are tied together is to keep the
sane ones from going home. His point, of course, is that
we need friendships to keep us focused on what life is all
about. Without our ties to each other—through our
Baptism—we can easily get lost and out of focus and lose
our perspective on life. But we *are* "tied together" by our
Baptism in the Lord, and He provides us opportunities
to relate with friends and acquaintances so we can join
the psalmist and "sing for joy and be glad all our days,"
even in the midst of the pain, loneliness, and struggles we
encounter.

Friendships do not take away our grief and sorrow.
Instead, they enable us to deal more positively and effectively with our troubles as well as our joys. Friends—
who needs them? We all do, beginning with the friendship we have in the Lord Jesus Christ.

FOR REFLECTION OR DISCUSSION

1. Who is your best friend? Why do you choose this
   person? What does that friendship mean to you?

2. To whom are you a friend? How have you been
   helpful to this friend in support, affirmation, and
   encouragement?

3. Intentionally thank the Lord for your friends today. Perhaps you may want to renew some old friendships from the past for support and encouragement.

4. "To have a friend, be a friend!" How is that phrase true for you? What difference does it make in the way you deal with others?

5. Jesus calls us "friends." What does being His friend mean to you?

Keeping Happy and Healthy as a Midlifer

There is general agreement that there are three causes of stress for most midlife men:
Fear
Uncertainty
Doubt
Together, F.U.D. adds up to a perceived lack of control which often provokes anger. People famous for anger include perfectionists, overachievers, and people-pleasers. Others of us get angry because we can't discriminate between petty irritations such as traffic jams and major challenges such as sickness in the family. We give all situations near equal weight and that causes us much stress.

Because stress is often brought on by feelings of being out of control, one of the best ways to reduce stress is to remind ourselves that we are in control—at least of our attitude. If we can't fight or flee our current situation, the next best thing is to "flow" with it. We can take a deep breath, remind ourselves that in 150 years none of what's bothering us today will make a lick of difference, and memorize the prayer: "Lord, help!"

We can also work on this Top 10 List of ways midlifers can reduce stress:

1. Get better organized. Knowing what we need to do and when might help ease the situation.

2. Live in the present. Forget the past, it's over. Make today the best day of your life.

3. Help others. Turning our attention to the needs and cares of others can help us keep our "problems" in perspective.

4. Laugh, laugh, laugh. To laugh at ourselves and our situations can keep us healthy.

5. Let other people "do their thing." If that rude driver wants to cut you off, if the music is too loud, just assume that your friend is having a bad day and let it go.

6. Give people a break. Put the best construction on everything that's happening in your life. Give people the benefit of the doubt. Continue to be an "inverse paranoid"—that is, convince yourself that everyone is out to try to make you happy today.

7. Monitor the self-talk that goes on in your head. Keep your thoughts pure and simple. Keep positive and try to hang around with friendly people. Keep focused on what's good, right, and appropriate.

8. Treat yourself right. You do need the right amount of sleep, exercise, and food intake. As the old saying goes, "If your body doesn't feel good, nobody is going to feel good!"

9. Use different words. Instead of calling something a "problem," call it an "opportunity." Instead of calling something a "deadline," call it a "finish line." Instead of calling something a "hassle," call it a "challenge." Renaming situations can relieve a lot of stress. See how many negative words you currently use to describe things, and take a new creative and positive approach.

10. Remind yourself that other people and things can never make you angry. Only our own minds can do that. Don't blame things for your stress. Blame your thinking.

And know that the best way of cutting stress is the realization that our Lord continues to love, forgive, and care for us. He took our stress upon Himself as He stretched on the cross. Our stress has been overcome by His resurrection. And for this we rejoice. And for this we give thanks.

In the midst of our daily stresses, we realize that we are forgiven even when we continue to get stressed out, continue to take ourselves too seriously, or continue to focus on the wrong priorities.

Keeping happy and healthy is for us midlifers a way to continue to share our faith and hope in the Lord.

FOR REFLECTION OR DISCUSSION

1. What are some other ways that you use to cut stress in your life?

2. What are the main stresses you are going through right now?

3. How can someone help you with your stresses? Talk to a friend about them.

4. "Name" your stresses in prayer. How do promises such as Matthew 28:20 help you to deal with your stresses?

Matters of Midlife, Marriage, and Family

The Wife

In the fading light of another Friday evening, our conversation often goes something like this:

Me: Do you want to go to ...

She: No, we tried that place last week and we didn't ...

Me: I didn't think it was so bad ...

She: Why don't we go to that whatchamacallit place.

Me: I don't think ...

She: Maybe instead of just going ourselves, we could get ...

Me: I'm pretty sure they're busy this evening, remember ...

She: No, not them, they don't like places like ...

Me: Well, then, what about ...

She: They said that they wanted to get together to play
cards not go to ...

Me: Then let's give them a call and see if ...

She: Do you really feel like playing?

Me: We could just go to a ...

She: I looked in the paper, there's not a thing on ...

Me: I think I'll read my book.

She: You go ahead, I'm going to get ready for ...

Me: Already?

She: Well, what else is there to do?

I had a job once as a waiter in a small restaurant. To keep from being too bored, I used to watch the couples that came in. I got pretty good at telling which ones were really married. Interestingly, it had nothing to do with age or how they were dressed or whether they were polite to me or not. Married couples invariably sat together in silence for most of the evening. But it was not the uncomfortable silence of that first date. Not that desperate silence when you are trying to think of something, anything, to say that won't make you sound like a complete jerk. The silence of marriage is a silence of sameness, a silence of comfort. There is just no need or desire to fill the time with words. It is the silence of comfortable dullness.

LOVE CAN BE LIKE A PRISON

"You are 10 minutes late," she said.

Ten minutes? Didn't she know that some men come home 10 hours late? Some don't come home at all. Some think they have to spend a major portion of their waking hours bonding with their buddies at the bar. Some are desperately battling against a clock in their heads that keeps telling them that they are running out of time to make it big or get rich or succeed. These guys hardly remember what the word *home* means. What's 10 minutes?

"I was worried about you. I wish you'd let me know when you are going to be late. How do I know what might have happened?"

Her fears again. Fears that something will go wrong, that I will get hurt.

"What's wrong?" she calls quickly when I sigh out loud. She thinks I am having a heart attack.

"I'm fine," I call back. "Not ready to check out yet."

"That's not funny," she says.

Those fears. Her fears limit me. Her future is haunted by the bleak specter of widowhood. She knows too many widows. They are lonely, broken, disabled. They grasp at the days and dread the nights. She clings to me. Her fears become a kind of prison for me.

My friend Herb found a way out of the prison of sameness that marriage can become after 20 or 25 years.

"I didn't know I was going to end up living with a crabby old lady," Herb said. "If I wanted that, I would have stayed with my mother."

Herb went out and found what he calls a "younger companion." Now Herb's on a diet. He's taken to putting stuff in his hair to make it look darker. (It looks like he brushed shoe polish in his hair.) He wears tight clothes and does a lot of smiling and rushing around trying to look energetic. He listens to loud music—the kind he thinks young people like.

Herb's wife called my wife. And they were crying together on the phone.

Herb's wife looks broken. She doesn't lift her eyes very often. She only speaks loudly when she speaks of him.

But old Herb thinks he's solved the sameness, the tiredness problem. Herb thinks he's gotten out of the rut and grabbed some of the wonder of his younger years.

But I wonder.

I think back on those early years of our marriage and I don't get all warm inside. Oh, we loved each other then. Physically, passionately, with an intensity that was exciting.

But the slide down to reality from the illusion of the honeymoon was no fun. We both had to get off our pedestals. We both had to stop trying to hide our faults. We both had to learn to give more and more. And it was not always easy. There was an edge of disappointment to those early years. We discovered that we could not fill all of our needs for each other. We could not solve all of our problems by love and good intentions. I could not make her fears go away by pretending to be strong. And she could not avoid trying to help me be better by pointing out my faults again, and again, and again.

Those first few years tested our commitment. They tested our love. They tested us and made us strong as individuals and made us able to be together through the 20 or 25 years. I wonder if Herb and his new friend have the strength or the determination or the commitment to do it.

"Herbie's so cute," she said to me when we met on the street. "He just loves to buy me things."

I think old Herbie is in for a tough time and an eventual hard return to the reality of trying to sustain a marriage relationship that has become as comfortable and confined as an old slipper.

MIDLIFE MARRIAGE—THE FACES OF TESTING

At midlife, after all those years together, marriage mellows. The issues that test the marriage are not those of the early years. The stresses come with different faces:

1. *"Is that all there is?"* The face of an empty future can haunt the "empty nest" marriage years.

   The man came for counseling. He was "unhappy," he said. "We've spent our lives raising our kids. I dedicated myself to my business. Now the kids are gone, I'm facing early retirement. My wife and I don't know what to talk about now that the kids are out of the house. I see 20 or 30 years stretched out in front of me and they look like a barren desert. There is nothing out there in the future that excites or even interests me. Is that all there is?"

   Too often in midlife marriage, the best of our times together seem behind us. We may find even conversation a chore. We've run out of things to say. Even when we do things together there seems to be a dullness about it. We remember the younger days, see people who seem to have broken into a renewal of their lives away from an old marriage. They make the question even more pressing: "Is that all there is?"

A Note on Depression

Depression can complicate this face of midlife marriage. Situational depression (as opposed to the medical condition called "clinical depression" that requires medical assistance) can be a result of moving through midlife. It can be brought on by lost jobs or opportunities, the sense of loss when the children leave, and much more. Depression can throw a shroud over the day and a cloud over the future. Depression tempts us to pull even deeper into ourselves and away from our spouse and others.

The first thing to remember about depression: It is not a weakness. Depression that makes us withdraw, lose our appetite, lose our sense of hope, feel distant from God, move and think more slowly is a real emotional and spiritual condition that needs attention. It can happen to anyone. Depression needs to be dealt with. When we are depressed, it is time to get a medical evaluation and to get help from those who will listen to us and encourage us. Depression, even in its mild forms, should not be ignored.

2. *"You know me too well."* The face of sameness can bring a sense of being trapped to midlife marriage. When we have been together for 20 years or more, we live with someone who knows us better than anyone else in the world—better even than our parents. That person knows our weaknesses (and may point them out to us). She knows when we are likely to fail, the situations we don't handle very well. She knows how we think and act. She sees through us. And that intimacy—an intimacy more intense than anything in the early years of marriage—can

make us turn away from those eyes that see us almost better than we see ourselves.

3. *"Do you love me—still?"* The face of uncertainty can be a part of midlife marriage. In *Fiddler on the Roof* the aging couple has a tender question for each other: "Do you love me?" The response: "Of course, I love you." But the evidence for that love is in the day-to-dayness of living together. Uncertainty about loving and being loved can make the midlife marriage even more fragile.

The couple in *Fiddler* were great friends. You could see a real love passed between them. Not that he was all tenderness, but they were aware of one another when they were in the same room. He touched her occasionally, as one would touch a friend. They left notes for each other, even though they saw each other every day. The notes always ended with an expression of love—and "thank you."

It may seem easier to take our love for granted. After all, we've been married for all these years. We spend our time together. We share everything. How could we not love each other? But unexpressed love can die.

The reporter interviewed an English gentleman in his 90s. His health was not good. His wife of more than 60 years spent a lot of time caring for him. The reporter asked, tongue in cheek, what they did in bed every night. The old man replied without hesitation, "Every night, just before we go to sleep, I tell her I love her. If I don't wake in the morning, I want those to be the last words she hears from me."

Perhaps not only the last words, but the first words as well. Unexpressed love is unknown love. God's love is evident in the marvels of creation and the miracles all around us. But God's "I love you" comes to us as a gift in Jesus Christ's life and death. There God's love becomes expressed and real. We know we are loved and can love.

Day to day love needs to be spoken.

MIDLIFE MARRIAGE—THE FACES OF HOPE

Though midlife can put difficult faces on marriage, some of the faces of our mellowing marriage are more welcome:

1. *"You are my best friend."* The words are not often said aloud, but midlife marriage can move into something even more precious than the love of youth. Midlife spouses can become real friends. My friend—who happens to be married to me—loves me, accepts me, cares about me. My friend likes to do things with me, gives me gifts that make dull days sparkle. My friend is there when I need a listening ear and ready to encourage me when I feel down. My friend is my treasure. My friend is my wife. And if my wife is *my* friend, I have the chance to be her friend as well.

2. *"I cannot think of tomorrow without you."* The sameness that can make a midlife marriage dull can also be the strength of our future together. We depend on each other. We lend stability and wholeness to each other. We have learned to live in the space together—and yet give each other the space to live.

We look into the days ahead and know that we will live them better and more fully because we do it together.

3. *"You are God's gift to me—still."* God continues to come to us in many ways. We can, even more in midlife, find God in the wonder of the world around us. We can find God in the majesty of great music or the pomp and circumstance of a well-crafted worship service. We can see God's hand in the miracles that touch our lives and see the image of God in the eyes of our children and grandchildren. But God's love comes to us most clearly in the patient presence of that wife who, though our faults are sometimes too evident, loves us in spite of ourselves. There in our relationship with her do we find the love that assures us that, in Christ, God can and does love "even me."

MOVING INTO THE FUTURE—TOGETHER

There is no easy time of marriage. Marriage is a relationship under construction—not just through our own efforts, but through the grace of God.

My wife and I took a walk the other evening. She took my hand and we walked in silence for a while.

"I love you," she said.

"Really? After all these years. After I've failed you so often and not always been the kind of husband I know you needed and wanted?"

"You are what I needed and wanted."

"Your folks never thought we would make it."

"My folks weren't always right."

We were quiet again for a while. Then she went on.

"I wonder sometimes if you aren't tired of me. Maybe you want to do like your friend Herb and trade me in for someone younger and more exciting. I know I don't look anything like I used to. My face is wrinkled. And the girl at the beauty shop asked me the other day, 'What color was your hair before it turned gray?' I'm nothing like the girl you married."

"I married a girl. A young girl with lots of dreams and lots of expectations. I know I disappointed that girl. But she stayed with me. I lived with a young woman who had lots of hopes for what our life might become. I know I disappointed that young woman. But she stayed with me. I live with a fine lady now. I know I sometimes disappoint that fine lady. I let her down. I take her for granted. I forget things I should remember. I don't always listen. But this lady will stay with me. I know that. And I promise this, my lady. I will never leave you. We have made something together that will last even beyond our years together."

We kept holding hands in silence. In comfortable, accepting silence. A silence that said more than our words had said. A silence that did not need to be filled with words.

FOR REFLECTION OR DISCUSSION

1. List all the gifts that your wife brings to you. Which of those are most important to you at this time of your life? Why? What gifts do you offer to your wife?

2. Read 1 Corinthians 1–3. What in that reading describes your marriage relationship? What remains something to strive for? When are you most aware of God's presence in your marriage?

3. What barriers to happiness in marriage face you? How do you deal with those barriers? How can you deal with those barriers most effectively? Who can help you?

4. What do you do to revitalize your marriage relationship? What actions or activities seem to bring you closer? How can you enjoy those activities more?

RESURRECTION ACTIONS

1. Sit down with your wife and carefully look at your relationship. Where are your strengths? Where are your weaknesses? How do you express love for each other? How can you build on your strengths and overcome your weaknesses? Plan several actions or activities (a weekend away, time every day for real talk, writing "heart messages" to each other every day) that can help your relationship grow.

2. Meet with another couple about your same age. Tell one another what treasures you find in your maturing relationship with each other. Make a contract to meet periodically with the other couple to share your successes and to encourage one another.

3. Give an unexpected gift and a thank you. See what you can do each day to make your wife smile.

Still Trying to Change Her after All These Years

You'd think I would learn. After 35 years of marriage, why is it that I still find myself trying to change my spouse? I guess I'm just a slow learner.

The objective of marriage is not just to "be happy." Rather, happiness is the product of a relationship that grows between two people. Perhaps one of the reasons many marriages end in divorce is that the main focus is on happiness and when that isn't achieved, one or both of the partners decide to move on to find someone else who will bring them happiness.

Remember the wedding vows? How could we forget? "For better or for worse, in sickness or in health, for richer or for poorer." I'm finally realizing that this is not a multiple choice statement. (If it were, I would have chosen "better, healthier, and richer!") No, the marriage partnership brings two people together to share their ups and downs, joys and frustrations, deaths and resurrections, yes's and no's, highs and lows, ins and outs, and everything in between.

A TREASURE CALLED FORGIVENESS

Couples experiencing midlife together continue to have points of tension and conflict. They're called sin.

And the only thing that keeps two people together is the fact that we live constantly in the forgiveness of our Lord. When I try to change my wife, I'm forgiven. When I don't listen or understand as I should, I'm forgiven. When I don't share my joys and feelings appropriately, I'm forgiven.

There's a story about a couple who had been married for 60 years and the old gentleman loved his wife so much that one day he almost told her. Yes, we are forgiven even when we fail to communicate our love and joy.

Or, what about the couple who decided early on in their marriage that if they would ever sense an argument coming on, the husband would simply take a walk around the block. And after 50-some years of marriage, they both concluded that all the fresh air the husband got on his daily walks was very healthy for him.

Part of the forgiveness process in marriage during the middle years is also centered on humor. Study after study indicates that one effective ingredient of a healthy marriage is the ability of both mates to laugh at themselves and at each other. It keeps us human. It keeps us vulnerable. It helps us to surrender our lives to the Lord and say, "Lord, I'm really in trouble without You!"

NOT TOO SERIOUSLY

Humor in marriage becomes a very healthy way of relating God's grace to each other. Humor is not to be used to laugh our troubles away or to ignore major conflicts, but rather to keep us focused on Who is in charge in the first place.

One family I know has developed a Top 10 List of rules for a happy marriage:

1. Never yell at each other unless the house is on fire.

2. Remember that it takes two to make an argument. The one who is wrong is the one who will do most of the talking.

3. Yield to the wishes of the other—as an exercise in self-discipline, if you can't think of a better reason.

4. If you have a choice between making yourself or your mate look good, choose your mate.

5. Neglect the whole world rather than each other.

6. Never let the day end without saying at least one complimentary thing to your life-partner.

7. Never meet without an affectionate greeting.

8. Work hard at trying to make life less difficult for each other.

9. When you've made a mistake, talk it out and ask for forgiveness.

10. If you must argue, argue naked.

Middle-aged couples have much to share with each other and with younger couples. Why not consider being a mentor to a younger couple? It's not that you have all the answers, but you certainly have some practical experiences and real-life stories to share with others. And while you're doing it, seek out a couple older than you and ask them to be your mentors.

The marriage relationship is so critical that we need help from others to keep focused and on target. The sign of a healthy marriage is not that everything is going well. (I especially worry about those kind.) A healthy marriage is one where both parties realize that they need the help and support of others around them.

Yes, after all these years I'm still trying to change her. But after all these years, the engraving on our wedding rings still says it all—even though it's a little faded and hard to read: "One for the other—both for Christ!"

FOR REFLECTION OR DISCUSSION

1. Recall some of the best times in your marriage. Share these stories with others.

2. Reflect on some of the "not so good" times in your marriage. What have you learned from them?

3. What are two or three areas in your marriage that need continuing work? Talk to your spouse about how you can deal with them honestly and openly.

4. Volunteer to be a mentor to a newly married couple. Invite an older married couple to have dinner with you sometime next week.

The Midlife Grandfather

Grandfathering is one of the greatest gifts for midlife dads. It is our chance to relive our childhood days, to try to relate to our grandkids the way we wish we would have related to our own children, and to thank God for the great gift of life itself.

Grandparenting can also help each of us be better parents. It allows us to become stronger support for our own children, the parents of our grandkids. And whether or not we live geographically close to our grandchildren, there are significant and special ways for us to relate to them.

Isn't it fun to see or hear your grandkids doing something that drives their parents nuts that drove you crazy when your kids did it? Revenge may be the Lord's, but it's sure fun to observe.

Among the best things that a grandfather can do are to love Grandmother and to model love, acceptance, and forgiveness with each family member. Grandfathers are the "keepers of the faith-stories" in the family. Grandfathers need to be intentional about connecting faith and life for their grandkids. And one of the most important things for us to remember is that we are the grandparents and not the parents. Grandfathering is a good exercise in observing (not telling how things should be done) and then encouraging and supporting the decisions of the parents. This is not always easy to do.

In our home we have set up some "grandparent rules." We tell the grandkids that we don't really mind how they behave and act in their own home (although we really do) but that in our home there are certain rules we follow. For example, there is to be no eating of any food whatsoever beyond the kitchen doors. And to help monitor this, we have set up an imaginary "electric wire" that "buzzes" every time food is taken beyond the kitchen. It is amazing what fun we've had with this "buzzer." It really hasn't gone off very much because the grandkids stay within the kitchen area during food time. As a matter of fact, Grandpa forgot the "buzzer" system once and carried popcorn into the family room when all of a sudden the buzzer went off, which sounded a whole lot like the voices of his grandkids.

It is also helpful for grandfathers to tell as many stories to grandkids about their parents as possible. Let the grandkids know how funny and strange and fun-loving their parents were when they were kids. The funnier the stories, the better. Show the grandkids that their parents were and still are human. I am still amazed at the number of teenagers who could never picture their parents as shy children. Grandparents can help the two generations tell stories to each other about the "good old days" and the "good now days."

Ask your grandchildren for their opinions. What should I do about this? Do you think this tie will look good on me? What should we buy Grandma for her birthday? Let them help you make decisions. It teaches

them collaboration and shows them that they are important to you. And they probably can help you look good
in some situations.

Relate your story of Jesus to them in natural, normal
ways as often as possible. Make your faith alive by telling
"Jesus stories," by reading the Bible to the kids, by wor-
shiping with them, by singing hymns and praying with
them. Let their theme song be "I Love to Tell the
Story." Isn't it great to see how little kids can sing and
tell the stories of Jesus? Help them continue to say and
do their faith. Celebrate their faith with them.

Think out loud with your grandkids. Let them get
into your mind and thoughts. Obviously we need to
keep age factors in mind, but it is so helpful for grandkids to hear and sense some of the joys and frustrations
that their own grandfather is going through. It helps
them to understand that it's okay to share feelings. It
helps them to see grandparents as real people with the
love and forgiveness of Jesus living and working through
them.

Make sure your grandkids "overhear" you saying
good things about them. Encourage, encourage,
encourage. Affirm, affirm, affirm. Those are keys to the
grandparenting relationship. It's amazing how small
affirmations can fill the grandkids' bucket and make
their parents feel pretty good too.

It's also helpful to pretend that there is little your
grandchild can do that is bothersome. Family psycholo-
gist John Rosemond, in his "Grandparent Guidelines"
puts it well: "Young parents tend to be anxious. They
worry a lot about the jots and dots, and they overact to

things children have been doing since time in memorial. Grandparents do young parents great service by being the counterpoint to all this anxiousness." Rosemond correctly suggests that grandparents must stand ready to be "human tranquilizers."

John Rosemond is the author of eight books on child rearing and family life including *A Family of Value* (Andrews and McMeel).

Traditions have become more significant to me in these later years. I really do like the way Grandma decorates the house for the various holiday seasons. Our traditions of Advent wreaths, opening of Christmas gifts, and taking each grandchild out for a "birthday shopping spree" are probably more helpful and significant to me than to most others in the family. We grandparents need to be gentle teachers of the way life used to be. Helping our own kids and our grandkids remember and celebrate their baptismal birthdays is significant. Planning special trips throughout the year, going on a camping excursion, or even to a neighborhood ball game can be very meaningful experiences. And as families continue to move further and further apart, it will become even more valuable to be intentional about bringing families together for special occasions.

Yes, grandfathering is grand. Whether the grandkids are just down the street or thousands of miles away, we can visit, call, E-mail, send love notes, develop videos, share pictures, and do things together. It will be helpful to the grandkids and will make our midlife years more enjoyable, rewarding, and exciting.

FOR REFLECTION OR DISCUSSION

1. If you are a grandfather, share some of the best life experiences you've had with your grandkids.

2. What are some ways that you can more intentionally develop relationships with your own grandchild or with children in your neighborhood or congregation?

3. Volunteer to be a "grandfather" to a child in your congregation or community. What gifts do you bring to such a relationship? What gifts might a child bring to you?

Living the Empty-Nest Syndrome (Or, Don't Look Now but They're Back!)

I remember reading about the relief and happiness that hits a family when the last child leaves home. I remember reading that it may be tougher on the mom, but it is usually exhilarating and of great relief to the dad. I remember dreaming about all the extra time and quiet that would prevail around the hallowed halls of home. I even remember getting exited about being in charge of the TV remote control again.

But my midlife years have brought me once again to reality. The empty nest is not what it's cut out to be. And let me tell you why—they come back! It's great to have your kids and sometimes their families return home for a brief visit. But more and more midlifers are realizing that after college or work or travel, some of our offspring return to the nest, sometimes with little notice and few plans to leave again.

I still remember the conversation around the supper table one evening when child number two came home to the nest to live—temporarily! He looked at his parents in all seriousness one night and said, "So when are you two moving out?"

It is good that he and his parents still have a little sense of humor left, but the point was well taken. The return of the "chicks" to the nest can bring temporary excitement, but it can also bring misunderstanding, communication problems, tension, and stress among all involved. I know now why Bill Cosby says, "The only living things that allow their offspring to move back home with them are people."

There is no one way to deal with our children leaving home, coming back, or even visiting. We love them, we miss them, and we want them to develop their own lives, as long as it fits our values and lifestyles. Tension occurs when there are significant differences in how they and we look at life.

One of the joys of the empty-nest lifestyle is that we can begin to enjoy our children more. Our relationships change. They are mature adults. They count. They have contributions to make. It's actually fun to be in a relationship with our own children and ask *them* for their advice and counsel. And they even make sense—it must be because of their upbringing.

The same goes for grandchildren. To be a grandparent restores your faith in heredity. What a joy grandchildren are—most of the time. Especially when they visit and can go back to their own home. And the task of midlife grandparents is to spoil the grandchildren as much as possible. It is just as appropriate to allow grandparents to spoil their grandkids as it is inappropriate to allow parents to spoil their children.

One of the joys of being a midlifer is to see at least some of your own values and perceptions of life being acted out in your children's lives. Sure, there are disappointments and struggles. But there is forgiveness and acceptance because God in Christ has first forgiven and accepted each one of us.

Hooray for kids! Hooray for grandkids! Hooray for empty-nesters! And even hooray for offspring who return to the nest!

FOR REFLECTION OR DISCUSSION

1. What has been the most satisfying experience for you in your relationships with your grown children?

2. What else needs to be done to improve your relationships with your grown children?

3. Do your grown children tend to be more like you or your spouse in terms of their lifestyle, behavior patterns, dispositions, and attitudes? How do you react to those similarities and differences?

4. Think of ways that you can share something significant with your older children during the coming weeks.

Where Did I Leave My Glasses? (And Other Silly Remarks Midlifers Make)

As a fun exercise, keep track of some phrases and statements you say during the next week, as well as statements you hear others around you murmur. Being sensitive to some of the changes happening in our bodies, our memories, and our lifestyles will help us keep a positive perspective on experiences that can otherwise be devastating, negative, and stress-producing.

The aging process causes changes in our hearing, in our memory, and in how we go about our various routines. But instead of blaming all these changes on "old age," a more positive approach is to recognize these possible limitations and be ready to deal with them in an open, honest way.

I saw a bumper sticker that said, "Now that I have all the pieces of my life put together, I don't remember where I put them." It must have been written by a midlifer. Here are some phrases from my own lips as well as from some very close friends:

1. *"Where did I leave my glasses."* (This may also imply that I think someone hid them from me.)

2. *"What did you say?"* Or just plain "What?" My spouse accuses me of having selective hearing, but it may just be that my hearing is not what it used to be. ("What?" is often accompanied by "Turn it up" or "Turn it down.")

3. *"No, you didn't tell me."* Unless dealt with light-heartedly, this statement can really cause friction and stress within a family. Perhaps the most important thing is to find out what I didn't hear or didn't say and forget about whose fault it was.

4. *"I thought **you** were going to take out the garbage!"* That simply means "Oops, the garbage sits in our garage for another week!"

5. *"No, I do not snore!"* I have finally learned that friends who snore cannot be convinced that they are making those awful sounds. Best to retreat to another room, or remind them at a more "favorable" time, or even nudge them in the ribs during an exhale.

6. *"Why can't you put the dirty dishes in the dishwasher?"* or a related question *"Why can't you put gas in the car?"* These tremendously important decisions could possibly make or break a marriage so they need to be dealt with. Or else, blame it on your own mother or father, or just agree that a couple isn't going to have harmony on every occasion.

7. *"Do we have to invite **them** to the party?"* This can,

we hope, be dealt with in a calm manner, unless *them* happens to be a mother or mother-in-law, or even the grandchildren.

And on, and on. Be aware of usually insignificant matters which, during the middle years especially, could grow into major battles. And don't focus on who is right or wrong, or fixing all struggles, but rather on love, forgiveness, understanding, and respect. Listen to each other as you share the bigger issues, concerns, and challenges of life. Let's not spend the majority of our time on minor issues so that we aren't able or energized to deal with the major issues together.

But let me ask one last time, "*Do* you know where I left my glasses?"

FOR REFLECTION OR DISCUSSION

1. What are some minor rubs and struggles you have with your spouse or other family members? How do you usually resolve them?

2. When a person politely or intentionally "accuses you" of causing some discomfort in one's life, how do you handle it? Are there better ways of dealing with it?

3. Talk these matters over with your wife and other family members. Instead of majoring in minor concerns, what are some of the major issues that you could spend more time talking about?

Of Parents and Promise

"Promise me," she said. "Oh, promise me you
    won't send me to one of those places."
Ah, this rumpled old lady,
    diapered and dour,
    spreading guilt-laden demands on my time
    and my patience.
Oh, God, how she loved me then ...
Back then when I watched her pour out
    her year-by-year life for me.
The wrinkles that track her tissue skin remember—
    stitches and dishes and a thousand battled baths,
    and trips to the store for my child-tantrum whims.
She could catch my tears on her fingers
        before they fell,
    and could bandage even my self-inflicted wounds.
She dressed me in the clothes she would not buy
        for herself,
    and gave me the timeless time she could not keep
        for herself,
    and always—always she held me up before God
    with heart sounds that were more than prayers.
And now I only glimpse her through pools of tears
    in her graying eyes as she cries again for the doll
    that slips away through the wheels on her chair ...
Now the treasure fades as a dimming candle,
    and as her fluttering hands
    clutch my weary fingers,

I promise her a future-past that will never be.
This day.
This same, countless day.
I lay my remembered mother in Your Savior hands.
And when the spirit of what she used to be
    escapes into the secret solace of her hope
        for heaven,
Then let the sigh that trembles myself be more
        than relief.
Let it also be a wondering thanks for the loving eyes
    that watched me grow
    and cherished me.
For I was her treasure-child then,
    lying sure in her ever-mother hands.
And in her heart so sure,
    that even now in the dimness of years,
She does not stop loving me.

                    Ted Schroeder

It is easy to lose patience with them—they seem so helpless now. It is easy to be frustrated with them—their demands are so unrealistic. It is easy to be irritated with them—they won't even try to change. And worst of all—in their feeble step, their failing body, their dimming mind—we see ourselves, our own future. And it is frightening.

If it is difficult to deal with grown children, it is even more difficult to deal with aging parents.

In biblical times, those who reached great age were looked upon with honor and respect. Their words were valued (Genesis 49), their blessing was vital (Genesis 27), their leadership assumed (Deuteronomy 3:18ff). The first to bless the baby Jesus were ancient Simeon and Anna in the temple. The growing new Christian church after the resurrection of Jesus appointed leaders called "presbyteros"—literally the "aged ones."

The world has changed. In our culture aged ones are considered useless, burdens, drains on public (read "tax") funds. Older people are discounted by the young and ignored or barely tolerated by most of society. One does not have to visit many "homes" for the elderly to get a clear picture of just what value the aged have in our society.

As the midlife children of aging parents, it is difficult to escape the negative attitudes toward the aged that we encounter all around us. It is difficult not to see our aging parents as useless, as burdens, as "problems" that we have to solve. It is difficult not to seek ways to get them "out of the way" or to find ways to care for them that will not demand too much of our time and money.

It is interesting to note that the very first of the Ten Commandments that deals with our relationships with others tells us to "honor your father and mother." The honor demanded by the commandment does not cease when we reach adulthood or even midlife.

But telling ourselves that we ought to love and honor our parents does not always help us overcome the frustration and fear that we experience as we try to deal with them. And the more infirm and demanding our parents become, the more difficult we find it to continue to "love and honor" them.

BEFORE IT IS TOO LATE

Over the years I have worked with many people as they planned the funeral of their aged parent. Sometimes those who did the planning had to come a long way to the funeral. Others knew the way to their parent's home or their parent's "home" very well. Many of these planners expressed regret that they had not said more, done more, showed more, given more when their parent was alive. I never heard one say, "I wish I had not spent so much of myself on my parent while he/she was alive."

The time to fill the lives of our parents is now. But the strength and the ability to do that giving will not happen merely because of better resolve. It will not happen because we feel so terribly guilty when we ignore our parents. It will not happen because we find gratitude in our parents when we do give to them. It will only happen when we are able to include God's love for our parents in our own hearts.

UNDESERVED/UNCONDITIONAL LOVE

Without a doubt our parents made mistakes when they were raising us. Without a doubt they have done things over the years that have hurt us or our spouses or our children. Without a doubt they continue to do things that make our lives more difficult, make us feel frustrated, make us angry. Without a doubt our parents are far from perfect. They may, in fact, not even deserve the things that they expect from us. We may have a "right" to the grudge we hold against them. We may rightly feel that they have failed us in the past. We may have a "right" to stay away, to withhold our love, to keep to ourselves.

But all of that fades in the light of God's love for us. God has a right to avoid us too. He has a right to hold our failings and faults against us. God even has a right to keep His gifts to Himself since we neither appreciate nor deserve them. But God loves with a love that is beyond accounting. God "so loved the world [read "you and me"] that He gave His one and only son ..." (John 3:16). God's love gives. It does not keep score. It does not require that we are deserving. It does not expect return. God continues to give in grace out of love.

We find the love for our parents, despite their failings and faults, in God's love to us and to them. What we are called on to do is nothing less than to live the love that we have received in Jesus Christ. When we live that love, we give our parents the honor that is required and the attention and care that they need. Only in reflecting God's love do we offer an eternal love.

THE POWER IS IN THE PROMISE

Jesus once said, "... whatever you did for one of the least of these brothers of Mine, you did for Me" (Matthew 25:40). He wasn't only referring to the people we run across in prisons or hospitals or along the side of the road. First among those who are "the least" are those closest to us, those who need our love and our care. We are not able to be perfect children in giving love, honor, and care to our parents, but we can see Jesus in them and respond to them as He would.

The apostle John records Jesus' interesting word choice to describe the Holy Spirit. Jesus promises to send the "advocate." Others translate the word as "comforter." The Greek word is "parakletos." Literally, it means one who "comes alongside, with a commitment to stay."

When we are young, we depend on our parents. We relate to them as children. When we are young adults, we no longer depend on our parents but may join them in various activities and include them in our own family life. Then they become more like friends. But when they are old, they no longer need children or mere friends. They need those who will be God's presence for them, who will be paracletes for them. They need those who commit to "come alongside and to stay there."

Our actions as paracletes for our parents may not be rewarding. We may gain nothing from our care for them—at least as the world measures gain. People will probably not even pay much attention to what we do— it is, after all, expected. But as we carry out our commitment to be paracletes to our parents, we learn what it means to receive and to give back the grace that God has given us.

FOR REFLECTION OR DISCUSSION

1. Describe what your parents have meant to you over the years. How were they instrumental in giving you a start in life? What gifts did they give you? What do you have to thank them for?

2. What did you learn about being a parent (positive or negative) from your parents? How does God's love and forgiveness in Christ fit into that learning?

3. God is often called "Father" in the Bible. In fact, Jesus refers to God most often as "Father." What does that name mean for you? What image of God does it convey? What does it mean for how we view our own parents?

4. Plan one action in the coming weeks that will bring particular joy to your parents. Share your plan with someone else. Then after you carry out your plan, share the result. What was accomplished? How was God's love involved in your action?

Corned Beef on Rye
(Or, Your Sandwich Is Ready)

Midlifers have been labeled "The Sandwich Generation." That's because we are often called to be in relationship with our children and grandchildren on one end, and our aging parents on the other end.

Now I don't know much about making sandwiches, but I do know that they can be a lot of work. But they can always be so very delicious! There are different ingredients to a sandwich, depending on our likes and dislikes. But the key factor is that all the components of the sandwich come together to make it one delicious-looking and tasty gift.

Sandwiches can be messy too. They can slop all over the kitchen, ooze onto your shirt, and even cause heartburn. So it is with the relationships we have on both ends of our family spectrum.

So what are we going to do about it? More and more of us will be in the position to take care of our aging parents, since we and they are living longer. The sandwich generation is here to stay.

So we need to seek counsel and guidance from others who are going through similar situations. We can't do it alone. We need to be realistic in terms of living arrangements, finances, health care, transportation, and all matters in between.

It will no doubt take more of our energy, time, and finances to keep the sandwich from falling apart. And as we deal with each situation, we need to focus on God's gift of life and how we can share that gift with one another.

As a sandwich generation, we can help one another by approaching situations prudently. A good system is to be aware of the situation, deal with it intentionally and promptly, consider all the various options, involve as many family members as possible, and continue to ask for support and help from others, both professional and personal. We model love and acceptance as we take care of those in our immediate family. And we may find ourselves dealing with many blocks, barriers, and misunderstandings, but the key to keeping the sandwich enjoyable and healthful is to deal with the situations in a timely fashion, pray to the Lord for guidance and help, and involve as many people as possible.

FOR REFLECTION OR DISCUSSION

1. Talk to your aging parents about how they want to be cared for in later years. Or, consider how you are caring for a parent now. What difference does that caring make in your life?

2. Talk to your own children about how you would like to be cared for later in life.

3. Find ways to connect your parents and your grand-children. How can you help them communicate more effectively? What does each have to offer as gifts to the other?

4. Discover ways to celebrate with those of the generation before you and those of generations behind you. What could that celebration mean to your appreciation for each other?

SEVEN

Matters of Muscles and Manliness

The Sport

I jumped out of the shower, thinking hard about what I had to do that day. Busy day. A thought flew through my mind as I caught the image of myself in the mirror: "Gee, that old guy is in pretty bad shape."

Then, suddenly, it came to me. The old guy in the mirror was me.

———

It was a busy Saturday at the golf course. We waited almost an hour for our tee time, and a couple dozen golfers waited impatiently behind us. The pressure was on. I knew I had to do well, to hit the ball like I used to on the college golf team. I strode to the tee with an air of one unconcerned with the challenge ahead. I swung the club a few times with the rhythm and authority I seemed to remember. In my mind I saw the ball arching out into the dim distance, spanking the middle of the fairway 300 yards away—like it used to. I addressed the ball. A hush fell over the crowd. All eyes were fixed on me. "Eye on the ball," I told myself. "Left arm straight, swing back slowly but keep loose, pivot, shift your weight, now swing through."

The ball ducked. At least it was not where I thought I saw it. The club streaked through its arc and lightly tapped the top of the ball on the way by. The ball rolled—well, actually it dribbled—off the tee and stopped about 10 feet in front of me. A titter swept through the gathered throng.

"I told you the old guy couldn't hit," someone said.

———

Instead of a barber, I went to a "hair stylist" for a change. My hair was not the sort of thing that generally needed a lot of styling, but there seemed to be so much less of it than I used to have. I thought that someone might be able to arrange it or pile it or fluff it so it would look like more.

"I'd recommend a perm and a rinse," the stylist said.

A perm and a rinse? I tried to quickly estimate the cost from the list of charges on the wall. I stopped when I got to $80.00.

"Do you think it will help?" I muttered.

"Oh, definitely. The perm will give your hair—especially these little hairs on top here—more fullness, and the rinse will bring back some of your color."

"Well, I guess so."

"Then tell me," he said as he swished around me,

apparently also adding up the dollars in his head. "Just what color was your hair before it turned gray?"

———

I slapped the lather on my face for a quick shave. Lots needed to be done today. What an irritation to have to scratch the hair off of your face every day.

I stared at the lather in the mirror and set to work getting it off as quickly as possible. Just as I finished, I checked for leftover whiskers. Suddenly an image came to my mind. It was a face I had not thought of in decades. There, staring back at me, was my grandfather.

He had been in his 60s when I was a child. He had been the consummate ancient one. With his sage advice and sometimes not-so-gentle instruction, he tried to fit me for adult life. He died more than 30 years ago. And yet, there in the mirror, I saw him again. In truth, I was becoming the ancient one.

CHANGE

Inevitably, midlife brings change. Our relationships change, our outlook changes, our life tasks change. But the change that confronts us most unavoidably is our changing body.

For all of us, without fail, these changes begin to happen: The print on the page in front of us gets fuzzier and fuzzier; our reactions slow; we find ourselves following our stomach as we walk; muscles that used to be defined seem to melt; skin hangs; spots appear, and—seemingly at random—joints, muscles, and tendons begin to hurt. We move more slowly, get out of breath more quickly. And much more. Without fail. As surely as the turning of the clock, our body lets us know that we are moving into the autumn of our life when the leaves change and things begin to fall.

Of all the midlife changes, this is perhaps the most difficult to deal with partly because it is so obvious and it attacks so closely our sense of ourselves.

COPING WITH THE CHANGES

Frank approached his 45th year with great dread. He could see the "ravages of time," as he called it, gaining on him. He set about to do something about it. Frank got a hair transplant, some kind of a "face lift," and a tummy tuck. Frank worked out furiously, ran incessantly, put the best coloring agent in his still-thinning hair.

Frank kind of bounces when he walks and smiles a lot. Frank really looks like an older guy trying to look like a younger guy. I wonder if that is what he wants to appear to be.

———

I used to think that these words of The Preacher applied to someone else:

Remember your Creator in the days of your youth,
before the days of trouble come and the years
approach when you will say, "I find no pleasure in
them"—before the sun and the light and the moon
and the stars grow dark, and the clouds return
after the rain; when the keepers of the house trem-
ble, and the strong men stoop, when the grinders
cease because they are few, and those looking
through the windows grow dim; when the doors to

*the street are closed and the sound of grinding
fades; when men rise up at the sound of birds, but
all their songs grow faint; when men are afraid of
heights and of dangers in the streets; when the
almond tree blossoms and the grasshopper drags
himself along and desire no longer is stirred. Then
man goes to his eternal home and mourners go
about the streets. Remember him—before the silver
cord is severed, or the golden bowl is broken; before
the pitcher is shattered at the spring, or the wheel
broken at the well, and the dust returns to the
ground it came from, and the spirit returns to
God who gave it. (Ecclesiastes 12:1–7)*

Now they speak to me. The specter of myself as an "ancient one," as a "golden-ager," as the one who will sit on the park bench and clutter the sidewalk in front of younger people trying to get somewhere becomes more pressing. And it can be a depressing image.

REACTIONS TO OUR CHANGING BODIES

Saying that the aging process is inevitable doesn't help much. We need to be aware that part of dealing with our changing physical self during midlife can include

1. *Grief.* We will probably literally grieve over the person we used to be. We may experience our passing from the vigor of youth into the midlife years as a death. We are aware that someone has died. And that someone is the person we used to be.

Of course, the easiest thing to do with grief is to deny it or try to ignore it. But grief that is buried inside has a way of coming back to haunt or hurt us.

When we find it difficult to look in the mirror, when we try to ignore pain or make believe that we have not changed, when the mounting aches and pains make us depressed and angry, when we avoid physical tests or competition, when we pull back inside ourselves and find a shroud has clouded our future activity, we are grieving.

Grief needs to be named and faced. We have to acknowledge the death. As difficult as it may be, we will want to lay to rest that person who we used to be. We cannot bring him back to life. We cannot fool ourselves or the world into thinking that he's still there. We cannot pretend or imagine him back.

Not easy. It is easy to *tell* ourselves that we have to accept the passing of our younger, more robust self. But doing it is difficult. It may take time. And it may take the conversation, support, and encouragement of others who are suffering the same grief.

2. *Anger.* Some of us are prone to anger anyway. Some of us have difficulty expressing anger in acceptable ways. Some of us find much of our anger focused on ourselves. And anger can increase as our bodies continually fail to be and do what we want them to. There is no rage as terrible as that which we feel when we have done some dumb, clumsy, foolish thing brought on by our inability to do what we used to do.

I remember golfing with my father. I was in my teens; he was in midlife. He golfed pretty well for a self-taught amateur. But as he aged and I got stronger, it became harder and harder for him to beat me on the course. I would inevitably outdrive him. And I could walk fast enough to find my ball and help him find his as well. On one particularly difficult hole, I managed to hit my drive across the water hazard. His stopped just short of the pond. He hit one ball with all his might and it went in the water. Then another followed the same path. Then another. And I remember him, with seeming calm, putting his club back in his bag, picking up the whole bag, throwing it into the water, and walking off the course.

The worst of our anger is not usually turned on golf clubs but on ourselves or on those we love. To be angry with oneself can be destructive, especially if that anger is constant or suppressed. Like grief, anger that is not dealt with can come back to haunt or hurt us. Very simply, we need to acknowledge the anger and to get it out in healthy ways. If hitting golf balls or tennis balls or swimming or running (no matter how slowly) helps us put that anger at ourselves away, we need to do those things.

Most certainly, anger that is turned on others needs to be faced and done away with. We may not be able to do that ourselves. If our anger is turned on co-workers or on our spouse or on anyone else, we need to seek emotional and spiritual help. A counselor, pastor, or a group of others who are dealing with the same kind of anger can be helpful. The worst thing is to let the anger go on, get worse, become more violent—until we do something that forces us to come to terms with it.

3. *Depression.* A real result of daily dealing with the decline of our body and physical aging can be depression. A "what's the use" attitude can come over us and color all of our life. Depression, like anger and grief, needs to be dealt with either medically or through interaction with others (see "A Note on Depression" on page 100). Like anger and grief, depression will probably not go away by itself.

4. *Fear.* In reality, the mark of age on the body is the mark of decline and death. Though we don't want to admit it, the truth remains that the inevitable end of the aging process is helplessness and death. That can be terrifying—especially at times when we have only our thoughts to engage us and only our dwindling years to count ahead of us.

Of course, our problem with fear is the same one that likely plagued us all our lives. "Strong men aren't afraid," our culture tells us. Strong men are able to handle their fears. They are strong in the face of things that would make the lesser fade and faint. Strong men are tough. They can overcome. They are in control.

That is, of course, a lie. All of us are afraid. We all come to those quiet times when we cannot control our thoughts and the truth that death is in our future and that it is coming closer frightens us. We cannot pretend it away. We cannot bluff our way through. When we look at the changes in our bodies, when we become aware that we are getting weaker and less able, when we come to the realization that the process of decline in midlife is irreversible, we are afraid.

As with grief and anger, we can try to ignore fear but it will not go away simply because we pretend it is not there. Scripture indicates one remedy for fear, and it has nothing to do with pretending to be stronger or getting a hold of ourselves, or bluffing our way through: "There is no fear in love" (1 John 4:18).

The only place where fear gives way is in loving relationships with God and with others. The place to put our fears is in the hand of God. The place to look at our fears, to acknowledge them, and to stare them down is in the heart of others who love us and can lift us up when our fears threaten to overwhelm us.

IT'S A MATTER OF ATTITUDE

This truth remains: We can approach the future with grief, anger, fear, and depression. Or we can, with God's help, go about it more positively.

Scripture tells us many things that are important for our emotional and spiritual health. But one truth often escapes us: God cherishes older people. Children of promise (such as Isaac and John) were often born to older people. Early celebrators of the Christ child were ancient Simeon and Anna. Noah was several hundred years old before he finished the ark. And the great reve-

lation of John was written when the evangelist was probably in his nineties. The fact that we tend to give up on
ourselves as we get older does not mean that God gives
up on us. In fact, the challenges to use our time and
energies on God's missions may be more real and more
possible the older we get. God never apologized to the
older people He called and challenged to great tasks:
Abraham, Isaiah, Zechariah, and Elizabeth, to name a
few. There is a fullness of life that God has for us as we
continue to hear the call and to respond to the great
opportunities for service and mission that still lie before
us.

I visited two elderly couples. Both were in their 70s.
Both lived in modest houses in a residential neighborhood in a small town. Both were reasonably healthy.

At one house, gloom covered everything. The couple
boasted to me that they had not spoken to each other
for months. She constantly fussed that he would not go
out and buy her the muscle rub she needed and he did
his best to ignore her as he told the stories of his life (not
their life together). It was a chore to visit that house.

The other couple was often not home when I came
to call. They were busy doing dozens of things that
needed to be done in their community and at church.
They often said that they were "tired" after helping at
the food pantry or on the CROP walk. But they always
did those things together and always came away from
them with a smile. Their lives were full of doing and
learning and growing. They looked forward to the trips
they could take and the next wonder they could learn at
the library or in travel. They were a joy to visit.

The difference in those two couples had nothing to do with their age. It had nothing to do with the color of their hair or the shape of their muscles or whether or not they could hit a golf ball anymore. The difference was in attitude.

If we fight against the coming of age; if we take ourselves so seriously that we cannot laugh at our failings or find humor in our stumbling; if we turn inside and feel sorry for ourselves; if we endlessly grieve what used to be and long for what might have been; if we turn our anger at what we think we have lost, on ourselves, on others, or on God, we will become the shriveled, miserable, internalized, and lonely old ones. We will become the ancient, bitter people we all have known.

But if we seek God's help to meet age with grace and a positive attitude; if we continue to stretch our minds and our bodies (despite the pain); if we look forward to tomorrow for the wonders it offers us; if we continue to laugh; if we keep our relationships alive and vibrant as we grow, we can be filled with hope for the future—the hope that God offers in Jesus Christ—a hope that lasts past aging and sickness and even death.

I once played golf regularly with a gentle man who was in his 70s. I was much younger and stronger. I could hit the ball over 250 yards. I could carry any hazard or par 3 green. George did not even use a driver. He played most of the round with a 3 iron and putter. But George hit the ball straight. Not far, but straight down the middle of the fairway. And while I hacked around in the woods and stumbled through the rough, George waited patiently for me in the middle of the fairway where he smiled and made his next shot right down the middle. George regularly beat me. He knew what he could do and he did it well. George enjoyed himself. And one other thing about George. I never, ever heard him say, "Gee, I wish I could hit the ball as far as you."

The years will continue to come upon us, mark us, and change our bodies. But they do not have to change our minds or our spirits. The years can limit us, confine us, and embitter us. But they can also open opportunities and set before us even more engaging challenges. It simply depends on how we meet those coming years.

Jesus once said, "I came that they may have life, and have it abundantly" (John 10:10 NRSV). That promise applies not only in our youth, but in midlife and beyond.

FOR REFLECTION OR DISCUSSION

1. How have you experienced the physical changes of aging? How have those changes affected you? What is your reaction to the realization that your body is changing as you age?

2. Think of one person who seems to be "at home" with his/her aging. What characteristics about that person allow him/her to be comfortable with who he/she is? What is appealing about that person? Describe that person. What does that person have to teach you?

3. What does it mean to you as you plan for your life ahead to know that God often chose and used older people for special tasks and missions? What task or

challenge do you feel God might be setting out in front of you? How can you respond?

4. If aging is mostly a matter of attitude, what specific things can you do to help make your outlook on the future positive? With whom can you interact? In what activities can you take part? What kind of people do you want to be around?

A RESURRECTION ACTION

Make it a point to spend some time with both a younger man and an older man. Choose people you do not know well. Take time to listen and to share with one another about life goals, dreams, expectations, and challenges. What difference in attitude do you find between the two? What can you learn from each about your attitude? What can you offer to each of these men as you listen and share with them?

If you have time, you might "contract" with each of them to meet together for several learning/ growing/sharing sessions. Read and discuss a common interest. Or just spend time in conversation about the past, the present, and the future. Concentrate your discussion on what God is calling you to do and be at this point in your lives and into the future.

The Warrior

There we were—a dozen of us—out in the moonlit woods. There we were, all of us done up in loin cloths (the mosquitoes were thrilled), gathered around a blazing fire. Drums thumped. Painted dancers (well, movers) cast eerie shadows. Some of the would-be warriors waved sticks. Everyone was shouting. Everyone but me. I stepped back from the gathering into the darkness to watch. These are grown men, I thought to myself. These are men who wear suits to work and sit on recliners in the evening to watch TV. This is not a college initiation or some kind of weird cult. This frolic is supposed to help us recapture our "essential" male spirituality—or so they told us.

We ended up out there in the woods because we were told that as modern males we have become separated from our "inner warrior." We were told that at least part of the cause of our heartburn, our anxiety, our depression is that we have denied the basic, fiery, armed, potentially violent, male-bonded warrior that comes to us from our ancestors. Our comfortable, compressed, controlled life shuts out that real part of ourselves. So, we were told, the way to a more comfortable acceptance of self, the way to a more peaceful movement through our days, the way of preparation for the plateaus of aging (including middle age) is to get in touch with the warrior within.

And so there we were, waving weapons, eating off the land, sharing, dancing, singing, and bonding like crazy. I suppose it didn't hurt anything. Some came away from the weekend feeling refreshed, they said. Some had a deeper understanding of themselves, they said. Some thought it was fun. Others found it a little bizarre. I guess I belong to the latter group. If there is a warrior in me, he is pretty well hidden.

When my son was about 12, he wanted to go hunting. We borrowed a couple of shotguns and headed for a farmer's field to hunt rabbits. Easy enough, I thought. We tramped around for a while and shot the guns at stumps. Then a particularly stupid rabbit hopped out into a small clearing about 10 yards from where we were shooting. The rabbit just sat there staring at us. We both raised our guns. There was a long silence. Neither of us fired. Finally my son moved a little and the rabbit hopped slowly away into the weeds. We looked at each other, my son and I. It was obvious we were not going to become great hunters. We returned the shotguns and bought a camera. If there is a warrior in us, he is pretty well hidden.

Though the warrior may indeed be hidden deep inside us, it remains true that modern men seem to suffer from a deadness of their spiritual side. Research tells us many drift from religion during midlife. Most seem to be on a quest. Many find the quest does not fulfill their lives. The need to know our inner self and to find the core of our spirituality certainly does not diminish in midlife. In fact, the need to find that solid center in order to build a sense of peace there seems to increase in midlife.

And to be sure, for all our modernization, the warrior still seems to be a part of us. Do you know any of these warriors? (Perhaps we see aspects of them in the mirror ...)

Cal the Competitor. Whatever it is, Cal needs to win. He's the kid who used to always win at Bible baseball in confirmation class. He could find a passage faster than anyone. And Cal will do anything better or faster. Regardless of the subject, he has already seen it, read it, or done it. On an outing, he will get there before anyone else. ("What kept you?" he'll say.) Cal hates to lose. When Cal is the Little League coach, he drives the kids crazy with winning. When he leads the neighborhood picnic, it has to be better than any of the others in the area. If he gambles, Cal will gamble on anything. Cal's warrior-self loves winning.

Dirk the Dominator. Dirk is big. His ego is big; his body is big; his voice is big. He even walks big—elbows out, like someone is playing marching music. Dirk leans over people as he talks to them. He parades his opinions as if they were written on banners. In kindergarten, Dirk drove the teacher crazy. It didn't matter what kind of attention Dirk got, just so he was the center of attention. The warrior in Dirk needs to dominate.

Bill the Bonder. Bill loves to be with other men. Bill is on the golf team and the bowling team and the ping pong team. He's a member of the Kiwanis club and the Bass Fishing club. Bill has a closet full of uniforms that he loves to wear as he attends this group or that group. Bill wants to belong; he wants to be busy with activities that put him with, against, and among other men. The warrior in Bill makes him a joiner.

Hal the Hunter. Hal has a collection of guns that would put the Pentagon to shame. He also has a collection of trophies that make his den walls look like a natural history museum. Hal loves to shoot. When he holds a gun, he seems to caress it. He gets a thrill out of destroying targets and matching wits with animals. Hal knows how to prepare for a hunt, how to stalk prey, how to get to the kill, how to dress the dead animal, and how to boast over what he has done. The warrior in Hal makes him a hunter.

All these men—and many like them—are being driven by the warriors in them. The warrior is that male side of ourselves that seems to lean into action, competition, being with other men. It is that part of ourselves that makes us want to get out in the woods, to hunt things, to be on the trail of something. It is that part of ourselves that needs to feel powerful, in control (of ourselves and others), to be in the winner's circle, to be the center of attention. Though some would condemn many of the features of the warrior, not all of his influences are bad. Competition drives most sport. The need to excel is a vital element in success. The will to act gets things done. But since action can lead to becoming a workaholic and competition can lead to compulsive gambling and the need to dominate can lead to violence, many men end up denying that part of themselves. That denial can lead to more anxiety.

The trip to comfort with self and reaching a spirit of inner peace may indeed include coming to terms with that warrior in ourselves. For some men, it means being part of competitive teams. For others, it may mean dressing in loin cloths and dancing around a fire.

Even in their milder forms, influences of the warrior can be destructive: A woman virtually abandoned by a man who is out doing his male-bonding things may run out of patience. Especially in midlife when the children aren't there to fill up her time, a woman may need more of a man's time and attention. Waiting for him to come out of the woods or to bowl a 300 game may not satisfy her.

Some men seem to sit on a great deal of repressed anger. Perhaps because they do not have a good way to get the anger out, they seethe with rage, strike out (at least verbally) when frustrated, make unreasonable demands of others, and withdraw into themselves at periodic intervals.

Some men (they used to be called "Alpha" types or "Type 1" personalities) seem to be driven. They lunge into the future. They seize hold of tasks and rush at them. They drive toward goals with dogged determination. They often burn themselves out.

And, even in midlife, we have to admit that there are some of these drives or urges or influences in all of us. The question for those of us who come at our spirituality from a Christian perspective is how can we get in touch with the warrior in ourselves in a way that is beneficial to ourselves, supportive of others and our relationships with them, and open to the grace and renewal that God has for us?

As we seek to move more gently into our later years, each of us needs to do some of the following to come to terms with our midlife warrior.

1. *Assess.* How much warrior living (competition, bonding, dominating) do we need? Are many of the things that we are doing simply habit, or do we have a need to do them? Are there ways that we can do those things in more creative, inclusive, and healthy ways? Can we hunt with our wife, for example, with a camera instead of a gun? Can we join couples teams? Can we get together with several other men for sharing and Bible study instead of feeding the mosquitoes? Can we use our time of male bonding not just to satisfy the warrior in us, but to grow intellectually and spiritually as well?

2. *Balance.* Though it may be true that we have to get in touch with the warrior in ourselves, if we do only that we will be out of balance again. The warrior may demand attention but so does the nurturer, the learner, the dreamer, the child, the mentor, the companion, the husband, the father, the provider. When the warrior dominates, we may end up destroying the relationships we cherish. We may put up barriers between ourselves and people we love and drive ourselves into more depression and anxiety because our life is out of balance.

3. *Plan.* We should be able to tell quickly when we are out of balance. If we spend all our time "earning a living" or "getting ahead," our life is out of balance

and the results will eventually bring us down—emotionally, if nothing else. If we spend all our free time on "warrior" activities, our life is out of balance and the results will eventually be destructive—to relationships, if nothing else. A plan, at least a framework for our activities, can be a helpful way to maintain balance.

As we look at the coming months, we can ask some simple questions:

☐ How much time will I spend learning, growing, dreaming, revitalizing, being a companion to my wife or children?

☐ How much time will I spend on my own needs?

☐ How much time will I devote to reaching out past myself?

☐ How much time will I spend growing?

The answers should allow us to put some balance into our lives and activities.

It may well be true that when we reach midlife, we enter a spiritual desert. The desert may partly be the result of having a life that is out of balance. The demands of work, of other people—demands to do the things we think we want to do—can put our life out of balance and cause us to be busy without being fulfilled. In that time we will want to make time for our own spiritual growth. Following are some time-tested ways we can find our center, balance our lives, and attend to our spirituality:

1. *Find a mentor.* A one-on-one relationship with someone who has been there can be an invaluable aid in moving along our spiritual journey. Our mentor should be someone we can trust, not necessarily a relative, probably another man. He should be a willing listener, a gentle advisor. He should be willing to go with us and grow with us. Meeting with him for a set number of weeks or months can be most beneficial.

   An alternative that seems to work better for some men is meeting with two or three others in a small sharing group. These informal support groups often go on for years. The people in such groups form a bond of trust and friendship that is quite rare in our busy world. For some, the support and encouragement, the listening and sharing, the prayer and growth that come through this kind of group are invaluable.

2. *Set a course of study and reflection—take time for meditation and prayer.* It's easy to test the need for study and reflection. Make it a point to be in the house alone. Turn off everything—TV, radio, lights, everything. Sit still for as long as you can stand it. How does it feel? Uncomfortable? That discomfort indicates a need to become more at home with self and more willing to spend time in reflection and prayer. Quiet times of personal and private meditation and Bible study or prayer have been part of the lives of the saints for centuries. We rob ourselves if we don't make use of this openness

to the work of the Spirit in our hearts.

It may not be easy. We are so used to being busy that the time spent doing nothing may seem unproductive. Best advice: Start small. Take 10 minutes at first. Make it at a time of the day when nothing else is pushing. Make it part of your routine so that it doesn't get dropped as soon as things get busier or more difficult. Extend the time as you are able.

It is essential to get into the Word on a regular basis. Choose a method of study that works for you—commit to a study that walks you through the Bible in a year; work through a topical Bible study; spend time in devotion with your family; and encourage each member of your family to have his or her own private study time. Find ways to incorporate your private study topics with your family devotions. We all know the importance of exercising the body; getting into the Word exercises the spirit.

3. *Set a goal for new learning.* In midlife it is easy to get a feeling that we know pretty much what we need to know. We function well in our jobs or professions. We hear little that sounds new to us. We fit into a life routine that we seem equipped for. And someone told us the lie "you can't teach an old dog new tricks" and we half believe it. Very likely the most lively elderly people we know refuse to quit learning, keep their curiosity alive, and anticipate new growth every day. That sense of wonder about expanding our minds and our insights is an important part of growing spiritually.

4. *Look for insight into self and others every day.* A great danger in midlife is taking ourselves and others for granted. We know how we react. We seem to know how our spouse, co-workers, and friends behave. There are few surprises. We walk a path of sameness. The problem is that the path quickly becomes a rut. Being open to what is new in ourselves and in others means being willing to listen beyond words, to look beyond surface actions. We must be willing to react in new ways to the same old situations, to take risks, and to surprise ourselves and others. Relationships that fall into ruts (even our relationship with ourselves) can die.

5. *Act purposefully.* In midlife, it is easy to drift. Our spiritual journey seems to be on hold. Our daily activity seems routine. Our needs seem met. Our challenges seem few. And so we drift from day to day. We do the expected. We find time for recreation. We kind of go with the flow. In the movie *Dead Poets Society*, the teacher (played by Robin Williams) had an important piece of advice for his students. In Latin he said, "Carpe diem" (seize the day). The advice is not only for the young. When we are in midlife, we know what a day is, what it demands, what we have to do to get through it successfully. We know how days go by. But we tend to let them flow by. Seizing each day is a way of making sure that we invite the Spirit to go with us as we act for some purpose in that day. Seizing the day is a way of making the day serve us and give us a sense of fulfillment. Seizing the day is a way of making

sure that what we do makes a difference and that
the accumulation of days amounts to a purpose.
The tendency in midlife is to drift until we run
aground. Seizing the day and acting purposefully
will lend direction and satisfaction to our lives.

6. *Attend a "spiritual renewal" retreat.* Many personal
   renewal retreats are available. Some of these are
   quiet and contemplative chances to meet with self
   and a mentor. Others are more structured and
   bring the retreater into contact with the spiritual
   experiences of others. All these can be beneficial in
   recentering ourselves and reassessing our values.
   Look for "crusillo" type retreats (some call them
   "kingdom weekends") and other opportunities for
   spiritual growth.

In truth, the warrior in us may be a fraud. It may be
that some of us (both male and female) have an inner
need for competition and bonding. It may be that some
of us enjoy the outdoors more or have a stronger need
to dominate. For some of us the warrior may be irrele-
vant. But the search to find our spiritual center and to
build a sense of purpose and peace on that center is not
a fraud. It remains a real and pressing need—even when
we deny it.

All of us are able to list the bad things that can happen in a man's life when he denies his spiritual needs,
closes down his inner self, and sets off in a self-serving
direction. All of us have seen the results of narrowed
lives that either drive toward a meaningless goal or drift
toward a rut of emptiness. It is not likely that our own

spiritual lives will suddenly become revitalized all by themselves. Renewal requires action.

Whether we take time for private reflection, meet with a mentor or in a small group, go on a retreat, or simply reassess our lives, some kind of action will be necessary to keep us growing spiritually through midlife.

Each of these actions, and others we might take, have benefit in themselves. But most important, they shut down some of the din of our rushing or the gloom of our drifting and let the Spirit dwell in us and speak to us. We know that renewal really comes from the work of the Spirit in the hearts and lives of those who gather in faith around the Word.

FOR REFLECTION OR DISCUSSION

1. Describe how you experience "the warrior" in you. How has the warrior been part of your life to this date? How do you experience the warrior differently in midlife than in your younger years? What is positive about that part of yourself? What is negative? What direction for the future do you discern as you contemplate the warrior?

2. Read in your Bible about the following warriors:

   Jacob: Genesis 32:22–32

   Moses: Exodus 14

   Joshua: Joshua 6

   Gideon: Judges 6–7

   David: 1 Samuel 17

Jesus: Matthew 21:12–13

Peter: John 18:10–11

What can we learn about being a warrior from these accounts? What is God's involvement with these warriors and their struggles?

3. Meet with another person who shows a maturity of faith and a comfort with self. What can you learn from that person about your sense of yourself, comfort with yourself, and direction for your spiritual growth? What can you share?

4. Write down a plan for your spiritual growth. Include assessment, balance, and action. Set out a way that will fit with your lifestyle and challenge you to new experiences with yourself and others. Share the plan with someone else and then do it. Reassess after you have completed the plan and continue planning into the future.

A RESURRECTION ACTION

Gather with two or three other midlife "warriors." Share some of the story of your recent spiritual growth. What similarities and differences do you see? What encouragement can you offer one another?

Make a commitment to meet together regularly (perhaps weekly) for several months. Talk about your hopes and plans for spiritual growth. Read and study Scripture together. Set out specific tasks or challenges that you intend to undertake and report the results to one another. Continue your group as it is helpful to you.

Too Much Going On and Not Enough Going Right

That was the response I got the other day when I asked a friend, "So how is it going?" And I had to admit, he identified some of my struggles along the way also.

There is just too much going on in our lives and often not enough that goes right. We strive, we work, we go the extra mile, and for what reason? We often feel that no one appreciates or recognizes our worth. We go through the various cycles of schooling, marriage, kids, earning a living, planning for retirement, grandkids, taking care of our parents, trying to make a living wage, and who notices? Or who cares?

Remember Peggy Lee's favorite song, "Is That All There Is?" She laments the fact that she too is going through all the stages of life but no one notices, and what difference does it really make?

Bob Buford in his book *Halftime* (Zondervan, 1994) says that "For the first half of our lives we strive for success—and the second half we strive for significance." Perhaps that is true for many people, but what about those of us who are still striving for success, even in midlife? Time is running out on the "Clock-of-Life," and we haven't even kicked a field goal. But before we remove ourselves from the game and take our place on the bench, let's do some reflecting on the "first half" of our lives. What do you feel best about up to this point? What have been your major accomplishments, your finest joys, your "touchdown runs"? It would be helpful to get in touch with these and share them with someone close to you.

And while we're looking at the scoreboard, let's take "time out" to reflect on some of our fumbles in life. What went wrong? What is something you really bungled?

What is it that you have been trying to forget all these years but still have in the back of your mind? I would suggest that, whether we feel like we're winning or losing the game of life at this "halftime," you and I are able to strive for significance in the days and years ahead. We are making a difference in the lives of people. We do this by sharing ourselves, our faith, our gifts with one another. Each of us has been given gifts and the task of using these gifts to care for and support other people.

A wise person once said, "Some people go around making a living; other people go around making a difference!" How has it been in your life so far?

Part of the problem with comparing life to a football game is that in football we have to do it all—we have to score the touchdown, hold the opposing team, make all the tackles. But in life, the Lord has freed us from worrying so much about getting to the finish line. You see, He has already taken care of that for us. And that frees us to spend less time worrying and thinking about ourselves and more time worrying and thinking about the needs of other people. Worrying, I believe, is not bad in itself, it's just that we worry about the wrong things. Instead of worrying about my life, my future, my mistakes, it's much healthier to "worry" about the needs of other people, the homeless, shut-in, lonely, and sick: "Religion that God our Father accepts as pure and faultless is this: to look after orphans and widows in their distress and to keep oneself from being polluted by the world" (James 1:27). We are called to visit, to heal, to be "Jesus with skin on" to the people around us. Talk about a significant purpose in life—wow!

I recently saw a button that said, "Jesus is coming soon. Look busy!" And that summarizes for many of us an improper relationship with the Lord. Surely He is coming soon, but that should free us to celebrate His presence among us now and not to worry about what we have left undone or still need to do.

You and I have made a difference in the lives of people. We have been given gifts to share with others, and we are simply asked to go through each day, making not only a living, but also a difference. Sounds good to me!

FOR REFLECTION OR DISCUSSION

1. What are some ways that you can encourage others around you to continue to strive to "make a difference" in the lives of others?

2. How do you deal with yourself when you don't feel very significant to other people?

3. List or reflect on some of your successes in life.

4. How can you be significant in the lives of others during the next half of your life?

EIGHT

A Plan to Renew Midlife Marriage

Marriages don't usually revitalize themselves. Like all relationships, marriages tend to become routine, taken for granted, and generally kind of dull. Midlife marriage can often be as comfortable as an old slipper and just about as exciting. A midlife marriage can come alive again, become exciting and fulfilling for both people, but renewal takes intention, commitment, and action.

The most important element in revitalizing a stagnant marriage is intention. If the marriage is going to come to life again, the two people involved in that marriage have to want it to and be willing to act in significant ways to make that new life happen.

The first step in bringing a marriage to life is *Renewing the Commitment.* To do that, we can

1. *Meet and talk about our marriage.* We might agree to a time and place to talk—not about the weather or the price of groceries—about our relationship. Marriage renewal starts with a willingness to talk freely and openly about where you are in marriage from the two points of view. The talk takes patience and a great deal of active listening until the partners can feel that they really understand how the marriage looks through that other set of eyes.

2. *Agree on actions.* We can write them down if necessary. What exactly are we going to do to help the marriage come alive again? What are we willing to commit to as individuals? as a couple? What steps can we take to intentionally move toward a fuller commitment? Agree and get moving.

3. *Stay with it.* Renewal doesn't always happen in 20 minutes. The first effort to revitalize a dormant relationship may fail. So might the second and the third. But if the relationship was worth forming in the first place, it is worth renewing.

4. *Seek God's help.* God is in the renewal business. God's grace is the fundamental way that we know the love that puts the past away and experience the forgiveness that makes it possible to start over again. There may be things in our marriage that are too painful to revisit. There may be hurts and disappointments that have festered for years. The only way through the "garbage" is by the grace of God. It is by God's grace that we are loved and promised

life. It is by God's grace that we can renew our love and rebuild our life together. Then we can use some of these strategies (or actions like them) to rebuild:

A. *Do a renewal get-away.* We might either attend one of the organized marriage renewal retreats (i.e., Marriage Encounter, Marriage Enrichment) or put together a marriage renewal retreat of our own. The important strategy is to get away from phones, distractions, obligations, and the like and pay attention to each other. We will want to avoid places where entertainment, TV, and nightlife intrude. In our retreat time together, we will agree to pay attention to

☐ *Assessment*—look at the present: Where are we now in our relationship?

☐ *Remembering*—a visit to the past: How did we get here? What hurts remain that need to be forgiven? What strengths from the past do we have to build on?

☐ *Affirmation*—What have we created, by the grace of God, in this marriage? What is good and strong and worth saving? What can be the foundation of the rest of our years together? What do we still love about each other and about being together? Say it aloud.

☐ *Recommitment*—We can simply restate our marriage vows or make a commitment or promise to each other—the commitment that forms the heart of your relationship needs to be stated clearly.

☐ *Looking to the future*—What can we look forward to together? What fulfillment can we find as we share our life? What new things is God calling us to? What brightness do we see in the years ahead? We should say them out loud and plan to respond to some of those challenges.

B. *Get into a mentoring relationship with another couple.* We might agree to meet with another couple (or two) for a specific period of time. Contract to share the strengths and the weaknesses, the growing places and stopping places of our life together. As we share, we can help each other see our relationships more clearly. We will be able to affirm each other, build each other up. We might study the Word together. In all, we will want to make our time together a time to look forward to.

C. *Get outside ourselves.* We can find a challenge we can respond to together. It might be an activity at church or service in the neighborhood— something that will involve us both and get us out of the rut of day-to-day living. Rewards may not be monetary but will be many.

D. *Develop a hobby or recreational activity we can enjoy together.* Whatever it is, we'll want to make sure that it is enjoyable and fulfilling for both. It can be something as simple as walking or as complex as photography. The point is to do it and enjoy it together.

E. *Agree to write each other a letter at least once a week.* The letter should tell feelings. It should reveal something about how each of us is making it through the days, what we are carrying that might be shared, what we are looking forward to, what we are dealing with that might become an issue. The letters are not occasions for complaining. They are places to reveal something about ourselves and to express our love and gratitude to our partner. We'll want to make time to read and share the letters.

F. *Develop a new pattern for spiritual growth together.* Do we have time for shared devotional time now? If not, might we try it? Do we read something together at bedtime? We might try reading right after a meal. Or, try praying aloud together for each other and for your relationship. We can set aside time to read portions of Scripture together or read and reflect on devotional material. We should strive to make our spiritual growth time together something to look forward to.

G. *Take a trip to our past.* We might intentionally revisit a place where we lived when we were younger as we remember cherished people and places. We might take the walks we used to or do some of the old activities. The visit will allow us to talk about the good times and the struggles we had when we lived in that place. It will also help us reflect on some of the strengths of our relationship that were begun as we lived there. This remembering visit can be a great chance to celebrate our life together in that place as we name our shared memories.

H. *Do again (or for the first time) some of the "little things" that brighten the day.* We might leave thank-you notes or give an unexpected gift. We might call our spouse for a date—even if it is just for lunch. We might seek opportunities to give an unexpected compliment as we take time to listen and encourage. We can renew our comfortable touch in public as we let others know of our love for each other.

I. *Do something extraordinary—a little crazy, maybe.* We might take a balloon ride together or go roller-blading or ride a white-water raft. It would be fun to go to a motel and see if we can make people believe we are newlyweds. We can find time to laugh like we used to laugh.

J.–Z. In our talking together, we might add activities, plans, actions, and suggestions of our own.

Then do them!

NINE

A Plan to Renew the Midlife Journey

The midlife spiritual journey can be difficult. The passing of time, the realization that death is drawing nearer, the decline of physical abilities can make the spiritual journey in midlife a trip into depression and darkness. Many men in midlife rush about, live for their work, withdraw into themselves, run after youth in an attempt to avoid dealing with their spiritual journey through midlife into old age. None of these denial actions will do anything but postpone coming to terms with aging. In fact, they may deepen the sense of depression and loneliness when age finally stakes its claim.

But that does not mean we are helpless before the ravages of the grim reaper (or whatever dismal picture language one uses). We are not cast into the darkness of midlife and left there to struggle into an even deeper and darker old age. All of us know those who come through midlife almost unscathed. In fact, even in midlife, they seem to be enjoying themselves. We all know those who happily arrive at their later years and seem genuinely joyful about their stage in life. What is wrong with these people? Or rather, what is right with these people? And if something is right, what can we learn from them about renewing our own midlife? Below are some of the lessons gleaned from midlifers who have come through the crisis (or the muddle) and come out on the other side with smiles on their faces, gleams in their eyes, and anticipation of what the future can bring:

1. *Accept.* Despite all the claims that new products, exercise, cosmetic surgery, and hormones will make one younger, gracefully moving through midlife means giving up the fight. Not that there is anything wrong with exercise, new products, or even cosmetic surgery. But if they are "weapons" in our strategy to defeat the aging process, we are on a track that will inevitably lead to frustration and failure. Indeed, there are many things we can do to slow the aging process. There are other things we can do to mask its effects. But there is nothing we can do to make it go away. The first key to making a smooth trip through midlife is to look at ourselves in the mirror, honestly assess where we are in our life stage, and accept that as the place where God has put us to live and work and grow.

   Note: Acceptance does not mean resignation. To arrive at midlife, plant oneself on the nearest couch, and vegetate into old age is not acceptance. Acceptance is simply the realistic realization of where we are in life. It is not a sign of surrender.

2. *Anticipate.* The quickest way into depression in midlife is to back into the future, eyes firmly fixed on the past. No matter who we are, how well we have lived, how carefully we have moved into our future, the past is filled with regrets, missed opportunities, failed relationships, guilts, mistakes, and more. Despite all the successes we may find in our past and the things we savor in our memory, our past is a place where we can quickly become overwhelmed with what might have been—with dreams and intentions and plans gone astray. Trips to the past that resurrect these things are trips into depression.

While it may be tempting to spend time reflecting on what might have been, the key to a graceful move forward is to fix our eyes firmly on the future and anticipate what still can be. The first time we hear ourselves saying, "Well, I'm too old for that ..." we should immediately respond, "Why is that?" Why should we be too old? Look around—people in midlife and beyond are doing marvelous things. Some don't write their first novel until they are retired. Some return to school, earn advanced degrees, learn a new trade, gain new skills, and much more. We will never be able to carry through on a new interest, aim for a new goal, or seek a new achievement any younger than we are right now. We are never too old unless we think we are.

Looking to the future with anticipation is a key to moving positively through midlife.

3. *Assess.* Midlife is a great time to take time to reflect on where we are, where we have come from, and where we are going. It is a good time to look honestly at the gifts that God has given us and the challenges that God has placed before us.

It is important, however, that this assessment not turn into an exercise in self-pity. It is easy to get into the "if onlys" or "why can't I be like ..." It is easy to collect our regrets and pick at them like old, unhealed wounds. That kind of assessment will do nothing but push us farther into the darkness that midlife can become. Of course we need to be honest about our failures, but assessment that leads to positive action needs to list and affirm the strengths, gifts, talents, and abilities that we have. We will want to take careful stock of our potential for growth, the skills we have developed, the things we have to offer to others, the abilities that are unique to us. We will want to be honest (not in a boastful way) about what we can do and what we can accomplish. That kind of positive assessment is the first step in coming up with a plan that can move us more positively into our midlife future and beyond.

4. *Aim.* Every effective renewal plan is only as good as its aim. Unless we are clear about where we are headed, we probably won't get there. Assessment that leads to a lot of random activity is only going to produce more frustration. Our aims need to be

long term and short term.

In the long term: We will want to spend some time with questions such as the following: Just where do I want to be as a person, as a child of God, as father/husband/friend 10 years from now? What do I want to be doing? What do I want to be involved in? What do I want others to be saying about me? Answers to those questions need to be as specific as possible.

☐ If 10 years from now I will be retired, what will I be doing? How will I be using my time? How will I be active in my faith life? Where will I be making a contribution? *And the follow-up:* What skills and knowledge will I need to reach that goal?

☐ If 10 years from now I am still a husband but also a father and grandfather, what kind of a husband/father/grandfather do I want to be? How do I want my loved ones to experience my relationship with them? *And the follow-up:* What do I need to be doing to make sure I will be the person I want to be for them?

☐ If 10 years from now I want to be able to travel, to walk distances, to garden, to golf, what activities do I need to be involved in now that will help to ensure that I will be able to carry out those activities in the future?

☐ If 10 years from now I want to be on a spiritual journey that maintains a close contact with God, that features a growing relationship with Jesus Christ, and is active in inviting others, what do I need to be doing now in study, reflection, and learning to be in that place in the future?

All the questions and answers can begin to form the long-term goals we set for ourselves. The vision of what we can be in the future will lend brightness and anticipation to the present.

In the short term: Again, it will be impossible to do everything at once. Even trying to do too many things at once can lead to frustration. A realistic, short-term question is what can I be doing in the next week or month to begin to move toward my long-term goal? Can I be involved in a mentoring relationship with someone? Can I get in a small group? Can I find time to take a course at a local college? Can I take more time for personal reflection and meditation? Can I start a plan of devotional "talk time" with my wife? Can I set out on a renewed plan of physical activity? The short-term plan should feature some things that are do-able. And we should set check points to assess how we are doing in the short term and set subsequent goals.

5. *Act.* The commercial says "Just do it." That should be the motto of midlife. By midlife we may have become expert at assessing the probability of failure in the face of almost any challenge. We know what we can do and what we can't do. We know our weaknesses and our failings. We may be tempted to

not even try anymore. We may be tired of "doing our part." We may be ready to "leave things to the younger ones." We may find a certain comfort in backing away from all the activity and moving into a more vegetative state. But vegetables that sit around rot. And without action, we will too. To act in midlife is not simply to get busy with a flurry of activity designed to help us not think about our stage in life. It is not to be busier doing more of what we have been doing. To act is to carry through on the intentions, the aims, and the plans that we have set out for ourselves.

6. *Ask.* Unquestionably, our plan of action will need to start with prayer that seeks God's constant forgiveness for the failures in the past and that leans on the promises of God to bless us and remain with us as we move into the future. Like everything else we undertake, success in spiritual renewal is not going to work if we only depend on our own good intentions and resolve. For this kind of activity we need the presence and power of the Spirit touching us and empowering us. God promises the indwelling Spirit and abundant life. God promises "My word that goes out from My mouth: It will not return to Me empty, but will accomplish what I desire and achieve the purpose for which I sent it" (Isaiah 55:11). His Word will accomplish His will—even in our lives. And Jesus assures us "And surely I am with you always, to the very end of the age" (Matthew 28:20). With those promises and with the power of God at work in us, we cannot fail.

TEN

A Retreat Design

Our Faith Journey through Midlife

THE GOAL OF THIS RETREAT

This design will help a group of four or more midlife men see their journey through midlife in a new light, grow spiritually as they study together, and shape the bonds of support and friendship that can sustain them in the future.

PARTICIPANTS

This retreat will be most effective if all of the participants are men at about the same stage in life—somewhere in or near midlife. The retreat would work with a pair, but four or more participants will enrich the sharing and enhance the learning.

THE SETTING

Ideally, this retreat should be done at some out-of-

174 Miracles in the Middle

the-way place that features space for walking, thinking, reflecting; a place that offers quiet and escape from phones, TV, and other interruptions. Someone's cabin in the woods or a quiet retreat center would be great. But if an ideal setting is not available, the retreat could be done in someone's living room, in the library or a quiet meeting room at the church, or any place that the group can get together for the discussion sessions.

PLANNING FOR THE RETREAT

☐ You will want to make sure that each person who will attend the retreat has a copy of this book. Get the book to them before your retreat, if possible.

☐ You may also want to arrange for meals and breaks, sleeping quarters, games and other activities, and materials to read during quiet time, etc.

☐ Make sure that participants bring along their Bibles and that you have plenty of newsprint, marking pens, note cards, paper, and pencils. One of the activities suggests the use of clay or newspaper.

☐ Ask someone to prepare brief devotions that can be used at the times indicated in the design below.

THE SCHEDULE

The following schedule envisions the group being together for two days starting on an evening and going through to the afternoon of the second day. For example, a Friday evening through a Sunday afternoon. You will want to adjust the schedule to meet the needs and the time available for your group.

Day 1

Evening meal together (Optional)

Session 1: Getting Started—Approximately 2 hours

☐ Opening Devotion

☐ Get Acquainted. Ask each participant to make a "name tag" (use large note cards or half sheets of paper) that includes: Name or nickname, favorite author or sports figure, most influential person from the past, favorite leisure activity, and work or occupation. Each of these items might be represented by a name, symbol, or picture on the note card. Each person in turn tells about his name tag.

☐ Read together the Introduction and "Who are These Men Who Live the Promise in Midlife?" from this book. Allow time for participants to read the material silently or read it aloud, asking volunteers to read paragraphs or pages. Talk about what you have read using the discussion questions provided in the book or the following:

1. What seems "true" to you in what we have read?

2. In what way do you consider yourself a "midlifer"?

3. When does it become most clear to you that you are in midlife?

4. What are your feelings as you think about midlife?

☐ Suggest that participants individually complete this sentence: "If I was going to have a midlife crisis, it would be ..." After all have had time to write, take time to share in pairs or groups of three or four.

☐ Closing Devotion

Assignment

All are to read and reflect on "The Cave," "Where Are You Going?" "What We Can Learn from Dogs, Cats, and Grandchildren," and "No Laughing Matter" before tomorrow morning's session.

Quiet Time, Reading, or Reflecting Time—overnight

Day 2

Breakfast

Session 2: Matters of Attitude—1½–2 hours

☐ Opening Devotion

☐ Getting Started: Ask all to write down one insight that they came to from their reading overnight.

Share these in groups of three or four. *What similarities do you see as you share these with the whole group?*

☐ Review "The Cave." Allow time for small groups to summarize the section. Use the four items under *For Reflection or Discussion* as you reflect and share.

☐ Review "No Laughing Matter." Talk about several of the items under *For Reflection or Discussion.* Ask, *In what way can midlife become more of a "laughing matter" for you?*

☐ Review "Where Are You Going?" Ask participants to list some of their regrets. Ask, *Why are our attitudes toward the past and future vital as we move through midlife? What can you share that will help one another build a more positive attitude?*

☐ *Follow Through:* Ask each participant to focus on one "resurrection action" from your reading or discussion to do during your quiet time after this session. Encourage all to focus on a specific task related to their attitude toward midlife.

Assignment

Read "The Sport," "The Warrior," and "Too Much Going On and Not Enough Going Right," before your next session.

Quiet Time, Reading, or Reflecting Time—Approximately 3 hours, including lunch

Session 3: Facing Age Grace-Fully—1½–2 hours

☐ Getting Started: Ask participants to draw two pictures (word pictures are all right) describing themselves at age 21 and now. The descriptions can include what they looked like, but also what they felt like, their attitudes, their sense of themselves. Share these, as participants are willing, in groups of two or three.

☐ Review "The Warrior." Use the discussion questions, especially the Bible study (item 2) to share insights. Say, *List some of the ways you experience "the warrior." How is that experience positive? How is it negative?*

☐ Review "The Sport" and "Too Much Going On and Not Enough Going Right." Use the discussion questions to think through and share insights. Say, *Share what it means to "put to rest" the able athlete from the past. Why is that particularly difficult? What can you share that will help and support one another?*

☐ *Follow Through:* Ask each participant to use some of the time between sessions to describe just what he wants his "image" through midlife into older age to be. How would he like others to describe him? What can he do to make sure that the image is clear?

Assignment

Read "The Way," "The Mountain," "Who Needs Friends? We Do!" and "Keeping Happy and Healthy as a Midlifer" before your next session.

Recreation Time—3 hours for activities, games, etc.

Quiet Time, Reading, or Reflecting Time—2 hours, including dinner

Session 4: The Midlife Journey—1½–2 hours

☐ Getting Started: Ask each participant to take a sheet of newsprint or large sheet of paper and plot his spiritual journey. The "map" can include important events (positive and negative), important people, and the like. When all have completed the assignment, share the journeys in groups of three or four. Ask, *What events do you have in common? What is God's part in the journey?*

☐ Review "The Way" and use the discussion questions to share insights.

☐ Review "The Mountain" and use the discussion questions to share.

☐ Review "Who Needs Friends? We Do!" and "Keeping Happy and Healthy as a Midlifer." Discuss the insights. Ask, *What practical help in moving into your future do you find? How can you share that help with one another?*

☐ *Follow Through:* Before the next session or overnight, ask participants to draw or plot their "vision" for their future. Where is their life going? What events are they looking forward to? Who will be involved? What part does God have in the plan?

Assignment:

Married men can read "The Wife," "Still Trying to Change Her after All These Years," and any other segments under "Matters of Midlife, Marriage, and Family."

Quiet Time, Reading, or Reflecting Time—overnight

Day 3

Breakfast

Session 5: Midlife and Relationships—1½–2 hours

☐ Opening Devotion

☐ Getting Started: Give participants clay, newspaper, or paper and marking pens. Ask them to make a shape or draw a symbol that represents their marriage and/or family at this point in their lives. These can be shared in small groups of three or four. Ask, *What common images do you find?*

☐ Married men: Review "The Wife" and "Still Trying to Change Her after All These Years." Use the discussion questions for sharing. Unmarried men might want to use one of the other sections under "Matters of Midlife, Marriage, and Family" for discussion and reflection.

☐ *Follow Through:* Married men: Plan several actions you can take to renew or revitalize your marriage. Write your plan down and share it with several others. Make an agreement to meet at some time in the future to check how you are doing with your plan. Unmarried men: Plan several actions you can take to renew or revitalize your relationships with those closest to you. Write down your plan and share it with several others. Make an agreement to meet at some time in the future to check how you are doing with your plan.

Session 6: Moving into the Future—1 hour

☐ Allow participants time to chart out a plan for their spiritual renewal. Read through and use the suggestions in "A Plan to Renew the Midlife Journey." As participants work through that section alone or in small groups, encourage them to come up with sets of both long-term and short-term goals for themselves. Share these plans with one another. Conclude the planning process with a time of prayer that seeks the Spirit's help and power to carry through with the renewal plans.

☐ Agree to meet together several times after you return from your retreat. Keep your plan and check on your progress. Schedule times for Bible study and prayer as part of your follow-up.

Closing Worship and Departure